CAMBRIDGE LIBRARY COLLECTION

Books of enduring scholarly value

Spiritualism and Esoteric Knowledge

Magic, superstition, the occult sciences and esoteric knowledge appear regularly in the history of ideas alongside more established academic disciplines such as philosophy, natural history and theology. Particularly fascinating are periods of rapid scientific advances such as the Renaissance or the nineteenth century which also see a burgeoning of interest in the paranormal among the educated elite. This series provides primary texts and secondary sources for social historians and cultural anthropologists working in these areas, and all who wish for a wider understanding of the diverse intellectual and spiritual movements that formed a backdrop to the academic and political achievements of their day. It ranges from works on Babylonian and Jewish magic in the ancient world, through studies of sixteenth-century topics such as Cornelius Agrippa and the rapid spread of Rosicrucianism, to nineteenth-century publications by Sir Walter Scott and Sir Arthur Conan Doyle. Subjects include astrology, mesmerism, spiritualism, theosophy, clairvoyance, and ghost-seeing, as described both by their adherents and by sceptics.

Spiritualism, and the Age We Live In

Catherine Crowe (1790–1872) was a successful author of fiction, non-fiction and plays, who moved in literary circles and corresponded with the prominent authors of her day, including W. M. Thackeray and Harriet Martineau. Her interest in the supernatural and the spiritual dimension, and her frustration with the narrow-mindedness of her generation, are evident in this work, first published in 1859. A strong believer in the possibilities of spiritual planes and of forces beyond contemporary human knowledge, she suggests that much is still unknown to the human race, and that the advance of scientific materialism may hinder the search for spiritual insight. Unusually for her time, Crowe also questions the literal truth of the Bible, suggesting metaphorical interpretations of scripture, and asks how modern miracles or prophets might be recognised, in a society so closed to the possibility of the physically impossible.

Cambridge University Press has long been a pioneer in the reissuing of out-of-print titles from its own backlist, producing digital reprints of books that are still sought after by scholars and students but could not be reprinted economically using traditional technology. The Cambridge Library Collection extends this activity to a wider range of books which are still of importance to researchers and professionals, either for the source material they contain, or as landmarks in the history of their academic discipline.

Drawing from the world-renowned collections in the Cambridge University Library, and guided by the advice of experts in each subject area, Cambridge University Press is using state-of-the-art scanning machines in its own Printing House to capture the content of each book selected for inclusion. The files are processed to give a consistently clear, crisp image, and the books finished to the high quality standard for which the Press is recognised around the world. The latest print-on-demand technology ensures that the books will remain available indefinitely, and that orders for single or multiple copies can quickly be supplied.

The Cambridge Library Collection will bring back to life books of enduring scholarly value (including out-of-copyright works originally issued by other publishers) across a wide range of disciplines in the humanities and social sciences and in science and technology.

Spiritualism,
and the Age We Live In

CAMBRIDGE
UNIVERSITY PRESS

CAMBRIDGE UNIVERSITY PRESS

Cambridge, New York, Melbourne, Madrid, Cape Town, Singapore,
São Paolo, Delhi, Dubai, Tokyo, Mexico City

Published in the United States of America by Cambridge University Press, New York

www.cambridge.org
Information on this title: www.cambridge.org/9781108027700

This edition first published 1859
This digitally printed version 2010

ISBN 978-1-108-02770-0 Paperback

SPIRITUALISM,

AND

THE AGE WE LIVE IN.

BY

CATHERINE CROWE,

AUTHOR OF THE "NIGHT SIDE OF NATURE," ETC., ETC.

" Seek and ye shall find."

LONDON.
T. C. NEWBY, PUBLISHER, 30, WELBECK STREET,
CAVENDISH SQUARE.
1859.

PREFACE.

HAVING been frequently requested by English and American friends to write on the vexed question of Spiritualism, I have at length resolved to do so, seeing, as I believe, that there is now a favourable opportunity of awakening the public mind to its importance and significance.

The opinions and hypotheses here advanced, may, perhaps, seem bold and unwarranted, but I believe that, upon strict examination, they will not be found wholly without authority. Neither do I think they can justly give offence to any man; since I do not insist on people's believing in Spiritualism; I only urge them not to shut their eyes to it; and, I hope, shew cause why each should investigate it for himself, and thus become qualified to form a conscientious opinion on the subject.

I have a strong persuasion that whoever follows my advice will find himself amply repaid for his trouble.

CATHERINE CROWE.

SPIRITUALISM,

AND

THE AGE WE LIVE IN.

INTRODUCTION.

THERE are many subjects which man has investigated with success and good fruit; whilst there are others, and very important ones too, which he thinks it useless to waste his time on, finding that they involve mysteries he cannot solve. There are others, again, which he disdains or neglects to investigate, holding them either unworthy the attention of rational creatures, or because they have failed to excite his curiosity; and, lastly, there are others upon which most people pronounce and entertain the strongest opinions, though very few

B

have so much as attempted any investigation at all, and with respect to which it would be difficult to find a dozen opinions entirely coinciding.

With regard to the first class of subjects, nothing need here be said; but with regard to the second, it may be answered, that the difficulty of the enquiry is not a sufficient reason for our abstaining from it altogether, because we do not know what we may find out till we try, and we do know how many things have been discovered that on a first view appeared exceedingly hopeless, and were pronounced to be quite beyond our reach. Moreover, whatever view a man may take of the government of this world, whether he admit a particular providence or only a general scheme, he can hardly help observing that man is progressing under God's guidance in the main; and that if one department of our nature is not so highly developed as amongst a small portion of mankind at a former period, yet we have gained much more than we have lost; because, without in the least undervaluing the æsthetical development of certain nations of antiquity, it cannot be denied, that morals, humanities, and religion, in which we have made some advance towards juster views, are the main objects of this earthly pilgrimage.

It would appear, from observation of the past, that there is a certain rate of progress ordained for us; that all things have their *times*, that is *for us*. All truths are as old as eternity; but when *our* time is ripe for it, God sends us a ray of light, which we usually endeavour to extinguish, as also him who brings it. In the latter object we generally succeed; but in the former we never do; we spit upon it and heap on it all sorts of rubbish to put it out, and when we find we cannot, we begin to fight about it. And this is evidently the design of providence; for if man, with his obscure discernment and clouded intuitions, was too eager in his reception of novelties, we should fall into many pernicious errors, and much time would be lost in the pursuit of them; a step forward in a wrong direction being much more dangerous than standing still. Theories and opinions, whatever they regard, fashion excepted, have a wonderful tenacity, and after a man has made them his own, and pub-

licly adopted them, are very unwillingly relinquished. It is fitting, therefore, that new ones
should meet with opposition, and be established
with difficulty. Accordingly, it is so ordained.
The battle may be long and severe, and many
perish in the fight who appear to us well worthy to
have lived to see the victory; but out of the conflict,
truth is certain, in the long run, to prevail—as
much truth as it is intended we should grasp at
that time. For be it remembered, we never see the
whole—the work is never done, the battle is never
fought out; there is a *guerilla* warfare ever sus-
tained, by means of which, little by little, new
territory is gained and old idols are cast out, and
new ones too; for with new truths, there come,
commonly, new errors, and while we are hailing
the God, an idol creeps into the temple un-
observed.

The work is never done; for God makes no
full revelations. He gives us a little light, and
leaves us to find out its significance and its value,
and how to use it. If he told us all it is desirable
for us to know, we should be living a miraculous

life, and, as far as we can see, a useless one. However that may be, it is clearly not his intention; he gives us a hint, and requires of us to think it out and work it out ourselves. We must multiply our "talent."

And we do think and work out these hints when we find our efforts to suppress them are vain; and out of the clash of opinions a modicum of truth is elicited.

This appears to be the plan of our Education. Life is a battle, and we advance by antagonism.

When, at length, our contempt and anger have subsided, and we begin to look with some patience at the new truth which has dawned upon us, and, especially, if it appear in any way likely to promote our material well-being, its progress to further development is generally rapid; at all events, as soon as its material uses are discerned, there is no scarcity of investigators; and then it is invariably found that this despised, and often persecuted suggestion, opens out into uses much larger and more important than could have been at all anticipated.

Every student of the past, and observer of the present, knows this to be the history of all new discoveries; and that the physical advantages, comforts, and conveniences we now enjoy through the attainments of Experimental Science, have grown and ripened out of these, at first, despised and opposed germs of truth sent us by God; for these truths, ascertainable by experimental science, and commonly called "our discoveries," are as truly God-sent hints as if we heard them with our outward ears announced by a voice from Heaven. And, doubtless, he has many more in store for us, which in his own good time will be communicated, and which we shall sooner or later examine, cultivate, and reap the advantage of, till man shall have attained a level as much higher than that he now enjoys, as is the difference between the speed of the express train of to-day and the pack-horse of our ancestors. For we are evidently creatures progressing to some great end, whatever it be.

The plan of our education, then, as I observed before, seems to be this—God, when he sees fit,

sends us a scroll, and says, " Decipher it, and you
will find a valuable secret ;" and at length—sometimes after repeated hints—we do ; and it is thus
we gradually make advances in Science and Art,
and their practical application.

But there is a department of knowledge which, as
far as we yet know, is not reducible to experimental
science, and in relation to which our ideas, inas-
much as we have any, are extremely vague and
unsatisfactory. I allude to the knowledge or
science of *ourselves.* Of our bodies, as mechan-
ical constructions or instruments, we have, within
a comparatively short space of time, learnt a great
deal ; but of ourselves, as composite beings, we
know absolutely nothing. We have added nothing
to the knowledge of the ancients ; perhaps we
have rather lost what they knew or suspected.
Metaphysics gives us words without any distinct
ideas, and Psychology is a name without a science.
The former was man's own mode of investigating
himself ; the latter is waiting till God sees fit to
show us how to set about finding out what we are,

and what is the object and end of our creation, or
incarnation.

I shall be answered, that these are ultimate
facts; that, like other ultimate facts, we cannot get
beyond them; and that we have only to do our
duty here, and rest contented with our ignorance
on those matters which it is evidently not intended
we should know.   But seeing the gradual progress
of all knowledge, who can venture to say this?
And a further acquaintance with our own nature
and God's designs regarding us, is not likely to
incapacitate us for doing our duty here, but quite the
contrary.   If we believed that all knowledge comes
from him, that all man's discoveries have originated in God's whisperings, we should not despair
of a time arriving when he may see fit to reveal
to us some part of that great secret which every
human being who reflects must yearn to know.

But the moments that man has to spare from
the clash and conflict of worldly interests and occu-
pations are too few to be wasted in hopeless specu-
lations.   Though it is very necessary that certain
individuals should comprehend the mechanism of

his body, he thinks the world goes on very well without this higher knowledge. It is true, it would be a gratification of his curiosity, but he does not see that he could make it practical; it would not contribute to his earthly prosperity, or put money in his purse; besides, when a man finds an *ultimate fact*, he had better draw rein, and not waste time in a vain endeavour to get beyond it. But I repeat, we know nothing about ultimate facts, or whether there are any at all. We only know that at present we cannot get beyond a certain point, or see how we are to attempt an advance; but we do not know that God may not see fit to put us in the way; and we do not know that the end of man's earthly existence is not the highest *knowledge* as well as the highest virtue; and if so, we may be sure that a comprehension, or rather apprehension, of God's greatest work will not be left out of the catalogue of our future attainments.

It is *possible* that the total ignorance which now prevails regarding our spiritual nature and origin is one of the unalterable conditions of our existence; but, judging by analogy, it does not seem

probable; and at all events, not knowing whether
that ignorance is to continue or whether it may be
God's pleasure further to enlighten us, it is at least
becoming that we should place ourselves in a listening attitude, lest he should speak and we not
hear.

To this it will be objected, again, that he *has*
told us all we are to know; that we have only to
search the Scriptures, and that we shall there find
what we seek. Perhaps we should, if we understood their real spiritual meaning; but do we?
Besides, we have no reason to think that on any
subject whatever God's revelations have, or ever
will cease as long as the human race inhabits the
earth, or that revelations supplementary to the
Scriptures, and tending to their true interpretation,
in regard to which men are still at issue, may not
be vouchsafed.

But meanwhile will those who profess to be
satisfied with the knowledge they have acquired, be
pleased to tell us what they know of their own
being, and of the object or end of their creation.
They have learnt that they are immortal spirits;

but that appears to be a knowledge as old as the world, and never lost ; since we find that the most ancient religions inculcated the same doctrine. But why this immortal spirit was clothed with flesh, and sent here to live out his little day in sin and sorrow, and then disappear from the earth, leaving aching and wondering hearts behind, who can tell us ? Or can they tell us what are the relations of this immortal spirit to this mortal body ? Or why this germ of the Divine is so peccable ? We are told, indeed, that the flesh is weak, but can flesh have any will at all but that of the informing spirit ? Can flesh think ? It does not appear that it can even feel ; for physiologists teach us that the seat of thought and sensation is the mind, of which we believe the brain to be the instrument ; but even this last fact is uncertain ; and beyond this, all we know is, that we know nothing, and that we have made up our minds to be content with our ignorance.

Religion, as it exists at present, is a matter of feeling, not of understanding, and we attend more or less to its prescribed forms, and are more or less guided by its precepts ; but we do not seek to know its foundation or what is man's real relation to God. We have happily, indeed, outlived the day when *Freethinker* was a term of reproach: and there are few amongst us, let us hope, so unenlightened as not to be aware that the essential of thought is freedom, and that without it there can be none. Those who are not *free-thinkers* are not thinkers at all, but merely the recipients of other people's thoughts, which they swallow with their eyes shut; whilst very frequently those from whom they receive them got theirs by the same process, and accepted them with as little examination. This being the case, not to think freely is to abjure God's chiefest gift—the Divine Light of reason; and to abstain from seeking truth in any department, as being either above us or beneath us —or more absurd still, *dangerous*—is to distrust and insult Him.

No truth can be above our faculties if He leads us the way to it; none can be valueless; and observation of the, apparently, most unimportant phenomena may be the first dawnings of a great science; whilst as for any truth being dangerous, it is only those who have never reflected that can entertain the idea. Truths, natural and spiritual, are God's facts, and the more we know of them the better we must be, and the more able to obey his will and fulfil our destiny. His truths cannot be evil, they must be good ; and if so, good for us to know. There cannot be an evil truth, for the essence of evil is falsehood ; and if while in search of truth man wanders into falsehood, his falsehood will have no vitality except there be a modicum of truth mixed up with it. If there be, the modicum of truth will survive, and the falsehood die when it has done its work ; which work is, not unfrequently, to assist in hatching and bringing to light the truth which it had concealed till it was ripe, or rather till the world was ripe to receive it.

It is very possible, nay probable, that the higher truths—those to which I now allude, psychological and religious truths—are not to be developed till a much later period of the world's history ; but that is no reason why we should not endeavour to make a beginning, and keep our eyes and ears open to every hint that may be dropped by our Divine Instructor ; or that each should not offer his thought as a small contribution to a great end.   As I said before, if there is a modicum of truth in it, it will live, in spite of the contempt and derision with which it may at first be met.   If it be wholly false, it will die, as it is fit it should.

God's ways are not man's ways.   He does not teach by authority, or influence men's minds to accept his truths by the power and splendour of his emissaries.   If we sought to enlighten our fellow-creatures in a foreign country, the last thing we should think of would be to select a teacher born under their eyes in a manger, and to choose his assistants from the poorest and most ignorant classes.   Yet, his greatest message was so sent ; for though the inner and spiritual meaning of the Scriptures may be lost, the external has survived, at once, to hide and to preserve it ; destined in due time itself to fall away and disclose the precious kernel of which it is but the husk.

By this mode of teaching, which offends our pride, and provokes antagonism, this selection of the humble and obscure for his messengers, we learn that we must help ourselves. God will not take the work out of our hands, and let us gather the harvest we have not earned. If we will not listen, we shall not learn. No voice from Heaven will awe and convince us at once. We must humbly watch for the low whispers and the glimmering lights he chooses to bestow, and use the faculties he has given us to interpret and develope them.

We contemplate with wonder the achievements of the last few years in the physical sciences, and we look with pity upon preceding ages, marvelling what life can have been without the appliances that are now of such easy attainment ; but have we advanced one step in spiritual knowledge ? Is not man as much at issue as ever on all that regards his highest and eternal interests ? What are all these sects, these religions, these hair-splitting disputes about incomprehensible dogmas and childish forms, but that conflict, that antagonism, which shews us that we have not reached the truth, but must seek it still ? We have no disputes about the moral laws. Without here entering into the ques-

tion of whether we know these intuitively, or
whether the knowledge is acquired, every human
being of moderate intelligence, however he may
obey them or not, or however he may pervert them
by specious arguments, must admit their validity
and their beauty.   People do not justify their bad
actions by alleging that they are right, but excuse
them on the plea of their weakness, or their necessities.   Even a fanatic, who is roasting his fellow-
creature for some slight difference of opinion on a
subject of which neither the one nor the other has
any distinct comprehension, would not deny that
" to do justice and to love mercy" is his duty, or
that it is the best rule, on all accounts, temporal
and eternal, for man to follow ; he would only
justify his act to himself and others, by arguing
that he was fulfilling the law by destroying a dangerous and pernicious heretic, and that he burnt
him for the good of his soul.   And this is one of
the great evils of religions as they now exist,
namely, that they pervert men's consciences.   All
nations, all sects, maintain theirs to be the only
truth ; and though they no longer burn, they hate,

persecute, and oppress each other as far as they
have liberty to do so.   Surely this is bitter fruit
to grow out of so goodly a tree, and must indicate
something wrong at the root.   If the root were
godly, the fruit would be love.

Now, all this clash and conflict, these religious
wars and persecutions, these virulent disputes,
social and even domestic, are generally about the
meaning of words in regard to which it is hopeless
the disputants should ever come to any agreement,
since there appears no standard to appeal to ; and
the smaller the point of difference between them,
the more their fury rages.   Doubtless there is an
essence of truth in all religions, and that essence
is the original heavenly ray, and by that ray they
continue to be vivified.   But in the first place, the
bearer of a new light sometimes becomes himself
unfaithful.   Ambition, the love of power, human
frailty, step in, and he perverts the gift he brings
to his own uses ; or, if he do not, mankind is so
prone to idolatry, that he is no sooner gone, than
they begin to think more of the messenger than
the message.   His name is never absent from their

C

lips ; his words and deeds are more or less truly transmitted, but gradually the spirit of them is lost ; they adopt his errors as well as his inspirations, and maintain them with equal acrimony, till the treasure itself might slip away altogether, but for the forms and ceremonies with which man invests, and, at length, overlays it, till the divine light can scarcely pierce the symbols with which it is encumbered.

Then what follows ? Whilst many take the symbol for the thing signified, and content themselves with vain forms and observances, with which they think the wrath of God is to be appeased, and Heaven to be won, others, perceiving the error, but unable to discover the underlying truth, reject the whole thing with indignation as absurd and utterly unworthy the worshipped and the worshipper : and these individuals, both the one and the other, spend their lives according to their natural dispositions and amount of intelligence, virtuously or otherwise ; little influenced by religious restraints, but guided by a more or less susceptible conscience and sense of right and wrong. There are others who, however dissatisfied with the structure as it stands, cry " Let it be ! How shall we govern the unintel- ligent classes if we loosen a stone in this tottering fortress?" And they tremble to touch the fabric, lest it should crumble under their fingers and dis- close nothing beneath.   There are indeed some, comparatively few, I fear, who contrive to extract from dogmas they cannot comprehend, a comfort and a faith in which they repose with confidence ; content to submit their understandings to an au- thority which they do not presume to question or examine ; who read the letter with the eyes of their teachers, but each after his own manner, finding, or rather feeling in it a blessing for him- self—something that he can assimilate and make his own, without in any way being able to explain or convey it to another.   These are the humble and faithful Christians whom we are accustomed to say " have the grace of God ;" and so perhaps they have.

Then there are fanatics of all shades, the fore- most men in the fight, urged on by such a variety of motives and impulses, intellectual and emotional, that they defy analysis. But two things appear evident; first, that all these classes, and others not enumerated, find in dogmatic religion just what they bring to it; and secondly, that it exercises a very small degree of moral influence; the hopes and the fears that are held out as allurements to virtue or determents from vice, being too vague and remote to contend with urgent present interests and temptations. The experience of our own criminal jurisprudence teaches us, that the inefficiency of the law is, in a great degree, due to its uncertainty. Only persons under violent impulses, nearly allied to insanity, would commit crimes if they were sure to suffer the penalty attached to them; but the chances of escape are so numerous, that every criminal plays a game of hazard, in which he trusts to his luck for a happy result. And it is not only what we consider the vicious part of the population to which this observation is applicable. Were it so, it might be alleged that these are ignorant, uninstructed, and thoughtless; or so thoroughly and inherently corrupt that they are incapable of, or indifferent to, any moral or religious considerations. But it is to be feared, that these last form but a small numerical proportion of those whose lives and daily doings are governed by expediency rather than by that rule of right which an actual living faith in the threats or the promises of religion must inevitably induce. The amount of lax principle, dishonesty, hypocrisy, and of every phase of unfair and double dealing, in every trade and profession, and in every department and relation of life, public and private, it is needless to dilate on. The world admits it, laments it, and practises it. People who go to church, teach their children the ten commandments, and flog them for telling lies or appropriating their school-fellow's slate pencil, governed by custom and expediency, have no scruple in resorting to the secret frauds of commerce or pecuniary speculation ; and would excuse themselves upon the plea that they must live, and that dishonesty is so universal that honesty cannot thrive.

But if a man, knowing the uncertainty of life, and that each day he opens his eyes on the light may be his last, really and potently believed what his pastors teach him, namely, that by perseverance in these crooked ways he was inevitably incurring an eternity, or even any lengthened term, of unspeakable wretchedness, which he might be summoned to enter on before the next day's sun arose, is it conceivable that he would remain unmoved, solacing himself by the fallacious argument that necessity constrains him, and that he is no worse than his neighbours? Would he not rather shut up his shop or abandon his palace, crying, "Away with it all! Let me earn my crust by the labour of my hands and the sweat of my brow, and let me bring up my children to do the same, that they may have no desires nor any ambitions to lead them into temptation; and if we cannot find bread, let us die the death of starvation, so that our souls be saved."

This is what a man would do who was thoroughly awakened to the conviction of a future state, in which an eternity of inconceivable wretchedness or unspeakable bliss, one or the other, was inevitably to be his portion; and this is what men, so awakened, *have* done, and occasionally do now, only that they generally fly from one error to another; giving up the battle it is their business to fight, and seeking a fallacious refuge in a life of asceticism, at once useless to themselves and others.

Nor can we wonder at the small moral influence of dogmatic religion, and the inefficiency of these promises and threats to make men virtuous, when they cannot fail to observe how little their pastors themselves are affected by them. Ambition, love of dominion, too eager desire for wealth and worldly advantages, jealousy, intolerance, are the characteristics of all churches; insomuch, that it is the constant care of wise governments to avoid throwing too much power into their hands. That church that has the most, makes the worst use of it; priests, of whatever denomination, are no better than other men; and religion is, in fact, rather an engine of government, and a reinforcement to the police, than a saving health to men's souls.

The governments so use it, and the governed so receive it. It assists in the maintenance of order and decency, and these being to the manifest ad-

vantage of every class but the worst, it must
be supported.   Religion is respectable, and there is
no getting on without respectability ; therefore we
must respect religion—that is *our own*, the church
we belong to ; for we have very little respect for
any other, because these others are not our instruments, but those of our rivals or adversaries.

On the other hand, it must be admitted, that
constituted as we are, *certainty*—an absolute
living conviction—of the awful alternatives presented to us, would be too dreadful for human
nature to sustain ; and accordingly we see that
this conviction, where it arises, commonly conducts
its victim to the lunatic asylum ; and it is natural
it should be so, for small, indeed, must be the
number of those who, when they examine seriously
their own position in regard to a future state, can
be intellectually and emotionally assured that they
are safe.   Nor can those who place the greatest
reliance on mediation and atonement feel themselves by any means exempt from danger ; for
whatever view they may take of those mysteries,
one thing must be certain, namely, that such a

bending to expediency as involves a perseverance in conscious misdoing, and the violation of God's laws, trusting to the chance of making peace with him at the end, must entirely nullify their claim to the expected benefit. I believe, indeed, there is a sect of Christians who profess, or individuals amongst them do, that they are of the elect; that what we call good works are filthy rags, and that they shall be saved by faith, whatever they do. Another body of Christians, I have heard, die assured of salvation, provided they have received the last offices of their church; whilst all, of whatever denomination, who rest their hopes in the atonement, make a merit of believing in its efficacy, pity or despise those who do not; and upon this merit of believing, found their claims to inherit its benefits.

But, in the first place, there can be no merit in believing anything whatever, and it is stultifying men's intellects to persuade them that there is. What appears to us credible, we cannot help believing to a certain extent; and what appears to us incredible, we cannot help disbelieving or doubting; that is, our amount of belief or disbelief in anything whatever, must be in proportion to the value we set on the evidence, internal and external, for or against it. This is a process of the human mind over which we have no control; it is irrefragably so. We cannot withhold our belief from what appears to us self-evident; we cannot deny a portion of belief to what appears highly probable; and so of the reverse. We must withhold it from what appears to us impossible, and grant it grudgingly to what appears improbable. But there can be no merit in either state of mind, whatever be the subject on which the judgment is exercised. Our decision may be erroneous, but if we have weighed the evidence to the best of our opportunities and capacity, the mistake is a misfortune, not a fault.

In the next place, believing any abstract or transcendental proposition is not so easy as people who do not reflect, commonly suppose it to be. *Accepting* certain dogmas without examination is not believing them; it is only shifting the onus to the shoulders of our instructors, and declining to

take it on our own; and that is exactly what the
Roman Church requires of its members; and, indeed, what *every* church requires; for, though it
is true that the Protestant retains the right and
privilege of examining into the reasons for the
faith that is in him, it is a privilege, the use of
which is neither encouraged nor generally exercised,
nor can be. Sermons and dogmatical works are
not disquisitions, nor enquiries into the truth of
the dogmas they teach. The arguments are all on
one side. The thirty-nine articles and the cate-
chism insist on certain things to be believed, and
people in general say they believe them, without
knowing whether they do or not.

I am not urging this as a fault in the churches
or their members; it is one of the necessary conditions of the existence of any church whatever,
and an inevitable evil in our present state of knowledge. Mankind have neither time, means, capacity, nor inclination, for investigating the highest
truths; and an investigation worthy of the name
would be a life-long service, without any assurance
of arriving at truth at the end of it. It is there-

fore inevitable that the masses of mankind must
take their religion from their pastors ; who, even
if they had leisure and capacity, have usually no
inclination to examine or question received dogmas,
or to subject themselves to the odium or penalties
of an imputation of heresy by wandering from the
beaten track.

I therefore repeat that the generality of people
who repose in what they call their *belief* in the
mediation and atonement, are, in fact, merely re-
posing on a vague hope that divine mercy will, in
some way or other, be extended to them ; and
that they shall, notwithstanding their perseverance
in certain misdoings, which, as the world goes,
they cannot afford or have no inclination to relin-
quish, at last escape that awful doom which their
church assures them awaits those who continue in
their sin, or do not believe its dogmas.   They thus,
at the same time, deceive and relieve themselves of
an insupportable horror ; for certain it is, that none
of us, even the best, could feel secure that he had
attained that required degree of purity which, even
with every aid of mediation and atonement, would

entitle him, when summoned from this world, to enter the Kingdom of Heaven. And even if any there be who have a conscience so clear as to give them assurance in their own case, what peace could any mortal enjoy, when it is impossible that he should have the same assurance for those most dear to him ? Every death-bed would exhibit a scene of mental agony and awful terror, instead of that calm relinquishment of earthly life, only disturbed by bodily sufferings, worldly cares, or the regret of friends, as I have been informed by physicians it now usually is.

Happily, God is more merciful to his creatures than man to his fellows, and relieves us of burthens incompatible with our existence. He has so constituted us, that what we cannot endure, we throw off, or die under, and so escape it ; and as it was his purpose that we should live our lives, and work out our destinies, he has given us an ineradicable fund of hope and trust in his goodness to mitigate the awful denunciations of his wrath.

But the consequence of the mass of mankind taking their religion from somebody else, and swallowing it like a pill, with their eyes shut, at least, without daring to open them wide, lest, perchance, they should see more than they wish to see, is, that religion becomes in the main a geographical accident, or a thing you succeed to with the other advantages or disadvantages of your birth; whilst the refuge people seek in lax-belief or disbelief, from terrors which would unfit them to live and act their parts in the world, nullifies, or nearly so, its moral influence : and without pausing here to inquire on what the characters of human beings depend, or how they are formed, it cannot be denied, that there are good and earnest men of all religions, and good and earnest men who do not profess to believe in any.

I mean, of course, dogmatic religion; for no one, I conceive, above the level of an idiot or a savage, which last class includes the unhappy offspring of the criminal populations, born and bred in physical and mental darkness, is without a religious sense of some sort, however little it may influence his life or engage his attention. Now, this uncertainty regarding a future life, the effects

of which on the human mind are analogous to the
effects produced on the criminal populations by the
imperfect success of the best-devised restraints,
although, in our present state of spiritual progress,
inevitable, is certainly very undesirable ; and it therefore cannot possibly be the will of our Creator that
this should be the ultimatum of our knowledge,
and that we should never advance to a higher level.

Uncertainty and imperfection are conditions in-
separable from all human institutions ; and the
measure of human alloy in our Churches and Religions may be gaged by their very imperfections.
But there can be no uncertainty with God ; to him
all must be known ; to him the immutable truth,
the past and the future, are for ever present. There
is no such thing as *chance ;* there can be no escape,
no refuge; our destinies are known and decreed from
all time ; and the decree is irrevocable, whatever
it be.

Now, it is not consistent with God's goodness,
nor with his designs, as we gather them from the
history of our race, that we should remain in this
state of ineffectual knowledge or gross ignorance

of what most deeply concerns us, namely, our true relation to him. It is very easy to say, he is our Maker, our Creator, and the giver of all we enjoy ; and that, as such, we owe him gratitude and obedience ; but we are entitled to know more than this. If we enjoy much, we also suffer much. In too many instances, this earthly life, as far as we can see, is anything but a blessing ; and it is very rare to find anyone, however favourably placed, who would be willing to live again through all the pleasures of the past, if he must take also the pains with them. The difficulties and sufferings, physical and moral, that beset most of us in this world, added to the awful task we are told is imposed on us, namely, that surrounded with temptations, and with radically corrupt natures, we are to resist a powerful and subtle enemy, who is unceasingly at work to destroy us, are conditions which convert the earth into a battle field, and render earthly life a struggle that only ends when life itself terminates ; and since when this period arrives, we are taught by the same authority, that we shall inherit the meed of victory or defeat, eternal happiness or eternal misery ; and since no one, even to the last, can tell—unless in such instances as it pleases God to impress a secret conviction and assurance of salvation on the departing soul, the reality of which conviction and assurance cannot be imparted to another —since no one, I repeat, can be certain that he has won the palm and escaped the dreadful alternative— I think it may be admitted, that human life, viewed in its true aspect, as far as we know of it, is anything but a thing to be thankful for. It would rather appear to be an expiation, or an infliction, for some foregone sin ; for it is vain and cowardly to say, that man—that is, *earthly man*—has brought this doom upon himself, and that the whole race is to suffer eternally for the disobedience of one or more of his progenitors. For, in the first place, if we venture, as I maintain we are bound to do, to examine this question by the reasoning faculties that God has given us, we see that such a calamity befalling us in consequence of the offence of Adam, or the Adamic man, must be very unjust ; for the calamity must be either the result of a special decree or it must be a natural

D

and inevitable result.   The first hypothesis violates
all our ideas of justice, and therefore cannot be the
correct one ; for if we cannot predicate that God
is just, it would be vain to search his ways or try
to please him ; and to talk of *occulta justitia,* and
assert that God's justice is not our justice, is only
a pusillanimous way of evading the difficulty.   It
is true, we do not know all the elements of the
problem ; but it is that very knowledge, I assert,
we are bound to seek.

The second hypothesis, namely, that the whole
race is suffering for the sin of their progenitors by
a natural law, as children suffer from the profligacy
or misconduct of *their* especial progenitors, is open
to the same and, indeed, further objections ; at
least, it could only be supported by admitting a
third hypothesis, namely, that the power of God
is limited, and that he is himself the subject of
law; which is a view theologists, at all events, are
not prepared to entertain.   But, in the meanwhile,
we believe that he is the origin of all the laws,
spiritual and temporal, that govern the universe, in
time, and out of time ; and that they all emanate

from his will and Almighty power; therefore, whether we are the victims of a special decree, or of a natural consequence or law, we must, in the present state of our theological enlightenment, look to God alone as the author of either. He pronounced the decree or made the law ; and in the argument, it signifies little which view we adopt; as, in either case, he must have foreseen all the consequences that would ensue.

The manner in which we are taught he modified or limited the effects of his own decree or law, it is not my province to discuss; nor does that circumstance much affect my argument either ; because the atonement only rendered salvation possible upon certain conditions, which conditions are evaded ; and which conditions, also, in the past and present state of the world, human nature being constituted as it is, must *and will* be evaded; and will continue to be so, until man has more enlightened theological views ; till he learns what he is himself, and what are his relations to God. It is true he *knows* his duty, for God himself has taught it him ; that message was sent eighteen

D 2

hundred years ago, and every intelligent being re-
cognises it at once, however little he may obey it;
he sees that it is God's truth and rule of life.
" Do unto others as you would they should do unto
you." There are no angry disputes, no bloody
wars, no bitter persecutions, to establish the truth,
or prove the error of that tenet; and neglected as
it is in practice, it has done and is doing much for
the world. It is a grand thing to have so concise
and simple a rule of life by which to try our own
actions, and which each can apply for himself with
unerring certainty; our passions and interests are
so conflicting, that it is difficult not to veer from
the straight and narrow way in the pursuit of their
gratification, while our motives and incentives are
often so complicated, that it is not easy to disen-
tangle them or avoid self-deception, where self-
deception is convenient. But here is a rule, applicable to all cases—Would you like it yourself?
Would you that he should do so unto you or yours?
—A rule which, viewed in all its ramifications, comprises the whole duty of man; exclusive of any
special duty which may be connected with his

personal relations to the Deity. And so useful is this rule, that everybody supports it theoretically, and claims that everybody else shall be governed by it in practice; the only exception he makes is in his own favour.

But invaluable as this rule is with respect to our fellow-creatures, and perfect as it is for ourselves, in regard to our consciences and motives, owing to our circumscribed perceptions it does not in application always exempt us from grievous and mischievous error; because we cannot foresee the consequences of our actions, and fatal mistakes are frequently made with the best intentions, especially by persons in authority, and those who have to deal with great interests and large masses of men.

Moreover, whatever may be the primary cause or ultimate end and object of this earthly passage, one thing is evident, namely, that we were sent here to work and to live by work; and that a life without work of some sort is utterly meaningless, and only excusable on the score of extreme ignorance of our duty. Now, God must have known that the inevitable consequences of this decree, in creatures constituted as we are, must be conflicting interests, jealousies, rivalries, and difficulties, which must not only engender bad passions, but must furnish motives for, and temptations to, equally bad actions; temptations which actually place great masses, if not *the* mass of human beings, in a dilemma, fatal to any but the most robust virtue. And so well is this understood and so generally is it tacitly admitted, that we continue to deal with tradesmen, and individually may consider them respectable persons, whose business transactions we well know would not bear daylight. We employ professional men who we are aware are much more intent on filling their own pockets, than in any way extricating us from our difficulties, or promoting our advantage, however important may be the interests at stake. We associate without disgust with these, or with sinners on a larger scale— speculators, who play a desperate game of hazard with other people's money, devourers of the widow and the orphan, and the hard-earned pittance of the poor! Heartbreakers, who live in abundance, and walk abroad with shamele s faces, whilst the victims of their wickedness, driven from their home, robbed of their furniture, their very beds torn from under them, seek shelter within the cold bare walls of a garret or a voluntary grave ; or, may be, find one provided for them at the public expense in the poor house or the Lunatic Asylum.

Politicians, too, whose public acts and private motives are freely discussed and pronounced to be selfish, dishonest, unprincipled, and injurious to the best interests of society ; we shake hands with them and smile in their faces, agreeing that the world is one great humbug, and that it is very sad it should be so ; whilst the pulpit declaims in vain, and the comic literature of the day makes a jest and a profit of the universal profligacy and pre-valence of false pretences.

That this is not a desirable state of things, and that it would be well to remedy the evil, all must admit, and will admit; for it is every man's in-terest that every other man should be honest and virtuous ; more especially as it is one of the con-ditions of his being so himself. Each will say, " If nobody cheated me I could afford not to cheat

others." But how is an evil so widely spread, so
gigantic in its ramifications, to be remedied?
Legislatures do what they can, but they can never
reach men's consciences; whilst the amount of ill-
doing that cannot be comprised within any judicial
code, and the uncertainty whether such offenders
as are amenable to the law, will be overtaken by
the penalty they have incurred, must inevitably
render their interference to a great degree ineffectual. They can never get at the root of the evil,
they can only here and there lop its branches.
Some people expect much from religion; but I have
already observed, and I think the annals of the
past and present prove the correctness of the assertion, that religion—whatever its efficiency in the
maintenance of decency—has but little moral influence on mankind in general; and whatever well-
meant exertions are used in that direction, however churches are subscribed for and built, and
however from curiosity or in search of excitement,
people may crowd to hear the Spurgeons of the
day denounce God's wrath against sin and worldly
mindedness, preaching damnation to their souls,

and painting in the most frightful colours the awful retribution they are insuring for themselves by their daily lives, it is to be feared that the number of those daily lives that are reformed, or even sensibly influenced, by these exhortations and menaces, is not considerable.

I have not yet heard how many of Mr. Spurgeon's disciples have relinquished their trades or professions because they could not compete with the dishonest people around them without being dishonest themselves ; nor of how many, amongst those in high places, who occasionally form part of his congregation, have resigned their lucrative offices, or have retired from the distinctions of public life for the same reason. But I apprehend the number is exceedingly limited, since no one instance, as far as I am aware, has yet reached the public ear.

Now this is a state of things, I repeat, that can neither be pleasing to God nor man ; and in this last fact lies our rational ground of hope, for if man were content with his evil he would probably be left in it. But he is not, he is reconciled to it, because it is his nature to be reconciled to irremediable calamities, while he laments it and seeks its alleviation. But he cannot find the way. While he patches it up in one place, it breaks out in another. The only engines of reform and improvement he possesses are religion, law, and education. The inefficiency of the two first to contend with the evil, I have already alluded to ; and with respect to the last, it is sufficient to · observe, that education, though it has a tendency to restrain people from certain kinds of wickedness, it rather augments the temptations and the facilities for the commission of other kinds ; and, besides, that it is not the offences or lax-morality of the criminal or ignorant classes that presents the most alarming feature for our consideration, but the misdoings of society in general—what is called respectable society.

Now, when man seeks to remedy his evil, and cannot find how to do it for want of knowledge, *I* believe—and it is impossible for those who believe in an over-ruling providence to think otherwise— that God helps him by sending him more knowledge. There must be a truth somewhere ; a truth,

which, if we were acquainted with it, would enable
us to contend with, and overcome the great moral
evils that beset us ; and would also assist us in
unravelling the theological difficulties and per-
plexities in which we are floundering, struggling,
disputing, quarrelling, like benighted school children, lost in the mist ; their leaders, each crying
from opposite points of the compass, that they
have found the way—the only way—that those
will infallibly perish who persist in taking any
other ; whilst each bewildered child blindly follows
the most familiar voice, and neither able nor willing
to take the trouble of investigating the problem in
which his safety is involved, casts the whole responsibility on his guide—a few excepted, who,
finding these guides cannot agree amongst themselves, resolve to follow none of them, but to stand
still and wait for more light.

Nothing is so common as to hear it asserted
from the pulpit, that God knows our wants, and
will supply them ; and if ever there was a want
that imperatively called for aid from Heaven, it is
the want of religious enlightenment—a knowledge

of that truth which shall make us all literally and
actually one flock under one shepherd.   That truth
that shall shew us what we are, and the end and
object of this earthly pilgrimage ; whereby, we
shall be forced, not only *verbally* to admit, but
scientifically to know, that we are the offspring of
the Divine, and that every man is our brother.

But how shall we find this blessed truth ?   In
what direction even shall we seek it ? Whether it
be hidden in Scripture or not, assuredly men have
not found it there, since religious differences, if
less bitter, are as rife as ever.   Men are fallible
teachers, and those to whom the interpretation of
God's messages has been delegated in all ages of
the world, have been, as has been before observed,
apt to pervert them to their own uses and benefits.
This is admitted of every church as a body ; and
churches, we must remember, are made up of individuals.   It is not, therefore, to any. church, or
any man or woman, that we must look for the
truth that we may be sure is to come sooner or
later.   God himself must tell it us after his own
manner ; and he will, if we humbly ask and

honestly seek.   To object that we have no right
to enquire into these high mysteries, that he has
told us all we are to know, and all that it is necessary for us to know of our beings, and that all
physiological and psychological researches have
proved such enquiries to be utterly useless, I repeat,
is altogether inadmissible.

In the first place, we have an indefeasible right
to investigate every question that presents itself to
our intellects ; and it is not only a right, but an
urgent duty, to investigate one that so nearly concerns our well-being here and hereafter.   In the
next place, as for God's having told us all we are
to know, we must remember, that so said the
Jews eighteen hundred years ago—" Have we not
Moses and the prophets ?" and if there is an over-
ruling providence, we have no reason in the world
for believing that his revelations, in one form or
another, will ever cease ; if they did, we should be
at a complete stand-still ; for, of himself, man
discovers nothing.   In fact, the idea that they ever
would cease, could never have entered into man's
head had it not been the interest of every church

in the world to persuade him of it. Moreover, we
do not know what he has already told us till we
thoroughly understand the Scriptures, and till we
have also completed our investigations of nature
and possessed ourselves of all the knowledge that
wondrous volume contains. This we are very far
from having yet done; indeed we have but lately
discovered the true method of attempting it ; and,
consequently, the hitherto ill success of our physiological and psychological researches with respect
to the great truths here alluded to, proves nothing.
At the same time, there appears little probability
that the researches of physiologists will ever lead
us to more enlightened views of religion, or to a
more effectual remedy for the evils incident to our
present state of spiritual knowledge; and as for
psychology, we have no recognised facts to work
upon, but such as slip from our fingers when we
attempt to handle them. Men's minds are so infinitely various, though agreeing in a few main
characteristics, that no one can thoroughly understand the mind of another, or convey in intelligible
language a distinct conception of his own, even if

he understood it himself; which it is the more difficult to do, that the moment we begin to introvise, we derange the conditions of the subject of investigation.

But I repeat, there is a truth somewhere, that it is most desirable we should know, and without the aid of which we cannot see any way out of the complicated difficulties that perplex man's earthly life; and it is distrusting the divine government of the world to think we shall not be helped to find it, if we honestly seek it. As I have remarked, an enquiry into mysteries which are supposed to be purposely withheld from us, and which seem impenetrable by our human faculties, and, indeed, are so, unassisted—may strike some minds as not only idle, but presumptuous. But God is no irresponsible tyrant who bids his creatures continue to suffer and sin, they shall not know why or wherefore, when they desire to mend; and who is offended at reverential researches into his being and their own. Whatever be our relations to him, we *are* his creatures; it is he that has placed us here, and has ordered the

aggregate of human life as it is. We may argue
about freewill and necessity as long as we please,
there is no escaping from this position ; and that
being the case, it is pusillanimous to deny that
he owes us the means of further improvement in
virtue and happiness; and it is an insult to his goodness to suppose that he will not furnish them
when the time is ripe ; and I think there are many
indications that that time is fast approaching. The
rapid advance of physical science without any corresponding progress in spiritual knowledge, together with the earnest and wide-spread desire,
especially in this country, to improve the moral
condition, and alleviate the sufferings of humanity—
a desire followed by tentative efforts too often
abortive, from the complicated nature of the evils
to be redressed, and the imperfections of the human agents necessarily employed—has brought us
exactly to that position and point of time at which
we may naturally conceive some further light
would be granted, whereby we may discern in
what direction we should turn, to find our way out
of the labyrinth we are in. More than that, we

must not expect, for we shall not hear a voice from
Heaven crying aloud to us to do this or do that.
It will be a far distant whisper, the low breathing
of which will only reach those who listen attentively
for it; but some will do so, and in time, others
will be induced to enquire ; and so the tidings will
spread and spread, till the material advantages and
spiritual instruction gradually disclose themselves.
For God's designs are never frustrated, nor is the
echo of his whisper, though it may die away for a
time, ever lost. However few may hear it at first,
however deaf the ears it may fall upon, it is still
borne upon the wings of the wind, surging up
again, here and there, as the currents are more or
less favourable to its diffusion ; till at length the
deaf hear, and wonder where their ears were, that
they had not heard that still small voice before.
Science has environed us with physical comforts
and appliances unknown, as we believe, to any former age. Education, and the pleasures and advantages of art and literature, are becoming every
day more widely scattered and accessible to all
classes ; but religion is, at the same rate, degene-

E

rating into an empty formalism, while its practical influence is almost *nil*. I say *degenerating*, for doubtless, there was a period at which, if our predecessors had little light, they had certainly more fire ; a fire kept alive by active oppositions and persecutions ; but these having ceased, as the conviction stole upon men's minds that racking their bodies was not the way to convince their understandings, the fire has smouldered away till nothing remains but the ashes.

Men are moral or immoral, but it is not their religion that makes them one or the other. Theoretically, they approve of morality and almost universally inculcate it ; but the greatest number sin, each after his own fashion, according to his peculiar passions, position, or necessities, only careful to maintain the exterior of respectability, and not to do more wrong than he can help. So they live, hoping that when they die, God's mercy will reach them, and they shall go to Heaven ; for do they not frequent the church, and in the appointed form of words exalt God's power and majesty, and cry with an audible voice to the Lord to deliver them ?

And when the end comes, they are either carried off suddenly, or, the mind and body enfeebled by illness, they are incapable of thinking or feeling any lively interest in anything but a cessation of their sufferings; and while the bystanders pray with more or less earnestness, and the pastor speaks fallacious words of comfort, and makes hollow and unauthorised promises of salvation, the departing soul takes its leap into the dark abyss, which is the open gate—to what destiny?—Who shall say?

Roman Catholics assert that Protestantism is a fertile source of insanity, because the right to en-quire sets many minds afloat on an ocean where they are tost hither and thither, and can find no anchorage. If this be so, such a result is not to be wondered at in the present unsatisfactory state of our theological knowledge; and probably, if there were more honest and conscientious investi-gators, the result must be proportionably more alarming. But, as I have observed, people in general have neither ability, time, nor inclination, to undertake an enquiry which, if fully and com-

prehensively carried out, would be incompatible
with any other occupation, and for which, indeed,
a long life would be insufficient.

It is inevitable therefore, that the generality of
people should take their religion from the mouths
of other men; and equally inevitable that, so
taking it, it should degenerate into a cold formalism, on the one part, and a means of living
and an instrument of power, on the other.

But as long as the salvation of men's souls remains a means of living, or an instrument of power
to any set of men whatever, we may be sure that
we entertain very erroneous ideas on the subject;
and, in short, are involved in a great degree of
darkness. Very few men individually, and none
as a body or corporation, can be safely trusted
with so awful a function. I need not expatiate on
the reasons; they are patent to every observer;
and experience shows that the danger of invest-
ing human beings with such an office is only
limited by the limits of their power.

Whenever it pleases God to awaken us to more
enlightened views of our relations to him, and to

let us see more clearly the meaning and purpose of this earthly pilgrimage, we shall find that every man is a temple to himself; that the salvation of his soul is an affair between him and God alone, and that when he seeks him he will not have far to go to find him.

In the meantime, our evident task—and this much is happily seen and recognised—is the diffusion of education, and the lifting as many human minds as we can reach, out of the mire of ignorance and vice, as far as with our present means we are able to do it; and I conceive that the grand move in this direction, of late years, is the natural symptom and forerunner of the new light, as also the divine preparation for it; and in the promotion of this object, as educators and moral teachers, the clergy, where they do their duty, are very valuable coadjutors.

And here let me observe, that however freely, and some may think, dangerously, I have presumed to give my view of the present state of affairs with respect to religion and its want of moral influences, nothing is farther from my mind

than a rash and fanatical desire to suggest the
overthrow of that which is, till we have something better to replace it. On the contrary, we
must cherish and use to the best purposes the
"ineffectual fires" we have, till they are gradually
and safely superseded by a brighter sun of grace;
remembering that when we first perceive the dawn
the noon will yet be far distant. All I urge is,
that while we work, we should watch also.

Religion, to fulfil our perfect ideal of it,
should be an emotion arising out of knowledge,
not a form founded on prescription ; and though
forms, when the spirit which they originally en-
shrined is dead, may to some minds present a
faint image of its loveliness, as a frame from which
a portrait has fallen and perished, might awaken
tender memories in a few beholders, whose mind's
eye would shew them the features that once were
there—they have no tendency to generate or revi-
vify the essentials of Religion, which are the emotions of the soul and its consciousness of immediate
intercourse with God, but the contrary ; and every
body acknowledges this of every church but his
own.

We cannot love because we are told we ought to love; nor can we truly worship at any man's bidding. Love is an emotion that cannot be commanded; and real thankfulness can only be awakened by a conviction that we have something to be thankful for. This earthly life, as I have remarked is, as far as we see, a gift of very dubious quality; at the best chequered with a great deal of ill, and in many instances it is, apparently, an almost unmitigated evil. Why then should we love or thank the Giver for this gift of doubtful colour? We may *say* we do; and doubtless some people may really do so at certain happy moments; whilst other few may be so fortunately constituted, and pass so prosperously through their journey, that they may feel they have enjoyed a certain degree of happiness and are thankful, come what may afterwards.* But we must admit that the preponderance of lives are a trial and a struggle,

* In the course of my life I have met with but *one* individual who was thankful for existence on the last principle, and that was the late Mr. George Combe; and with but *one* only of mature age, who expressed himself willing to live his life over again, and that was Lord Jeffrey.

with short intermissions from beginning to end;
and that, without taking into account the doubtful
future, they are passages of pain and sorrow,
more or less, to all; and when we do drop into
the scale the extreme uncertainty of how far we
may escape hereafter the awful penalty denounced
against our shortcomings, it would be difficult to
prove, from anything we know at present, that life
is a benefit. We are, therefore, not in a situation
truly to worship God—or rather to love him, for
love, and the obedience that springs from love, is
the only worship that *can* be acceptable to him.
All the rest is a mockery; and I think if we
would only leave off stultifying ourselves and our
fellow-creatures, and could once look this subject
straight in the face, it would appear as evident as
the noonday sun, that there is an imperative demand for more light; and that what we have to
do, is not to dispute about incomprehensible
dogmas and senseless forms, but humbly and re-
verently to beseech God to grant us what is so
needful for us; and to seek, in every direction,
whether perchance he has not already bethought

him of our necessities, and whether there be not
somewhere, the dawn of á brighter day to be de-
scried.

Pale, distant, remote, it will assuredly first appear ; for, judging from the past, such we may
pronounce to be God's method of teaching us.
It will not glare in our faces, no trumpet will
announce its approach.   It may steal upon us
" like a thief in the night," and never wake us
from our slumbers ; but one thing in regard to it
is certain : namely, that when it does come, it will
not be by the wise men of the earth it will be
recognised, but by the foolish ones ; "for the
wisdom of this world is foolishness with God,"
who hath chosen " the foolish things of the world
to confound the wise ; and the weak things of the
world to confound the things that are mighty."

SEQUEL.

HAVING so far attempted to establish that there is
an imperative need of more light, or in other words,
a further revelation, to enable us to extricate ourselves from difficulties insurmountable in the present
state of our knowledge, and to " show us the path
of life," I will now cast a cursory glance over the
past and the present, and endeavour to discern
whether there be any indications of the direction
in which we are to seek it ; for seek we must if
we wish to find ; the labour and the pains will
assuredly not be spared us.

Nothing is more common than to hear people
—especially religious people—assert, I know not
on what authority that miracles have ceased.
Surely they must be very ill observers of nature
and human life that can make such an assertion,
when they are surrounded by daily miracles of

every kind and form, of the most astounding and
incomprehensible description, and which they only
fail to consider with wonder and awe, on account
of their multiplicity and constant or frequent re-
currence.   A miracle is understood to be an effect
without a cause, that is, that not being able to
discern any cause for the effect, we either repudiate
it or attribute it to the direct and special intervention of the Deity.   Now, a very little reflection
will shew us that this supposed characteristic of a
miracle is applicable to thousands of phenomena
that we witness every day of our lives, without
their exciting the least surprise.   Secondary causes
we can often trace, as where we plant an acorn we
know that, other conditions being favourable, an
oak will spring from it; but how it should do so
we have not the least conception.   We are accustomed to say it is a " law of nature," and think
no more about it.   Again, it has been lately discovered, that if we extend a wire betwixt one
place and another, and perform certain operations,
a message can be conveyed with almost the celerity
of lightning to any distance; and we call this a

valuable discovery, as no doubt the planting of an acorn was pronounced to be when that operation was first performed with the view to the production of an oak. But, in either instance, the part we play in the process is extremely small. We have simply discovered, that under certain conditions, such and such results follow ; and that these surprising results are what we call " Laws of Nature," the operation of which we have it in our power to call into action by supplying the necessary conditions. But as we know not wherefore, or how, out of that little acorn should proceed a magnificent tree, with its far-spreading roots, lofty stem, forest of leaves, bower of blossoms and edible fruit, neither do we know how, by the approximation of certain metallic agents, a power should be evolved that mysteriously conveys our thoughts and wishes to the other end of the world. Moreover, we know not what that power is, we never saw it, and only judge that there is such a power by its effects ; but, as in both these instances, and thousands of similar ones, we perceive the secondary causes of these results, we do not call them miracles, but laws of nature,

Now, what do we mean by a law of nature? I believe we mean either an unvarying result of some law, of which law we may know little or nothing more than its effects, and which effects we can therefore neither promote nor retard—for example, the rising and the setting of the sun; or else we mean one of those unvarying results which we can, in some degree, promote or retard, because we have discovered some of the necessary conditions or secondary causes, and are able with more or less certainty to apply them; as in the planting of an acorn or preparing a telegraphic apparatus. But of the first result, the rising and the setting of the sun, we know little or nothing but that it is the will of God that it should be so; and the only reason we do not call it a miracle but a law of nature, is, that as far as we know it has always risen and set with the same regularity, and we presume that it always will do so. With respect to those laws of nature that are included in the second category, as the springing of the oak, and the despatch of the message, we are almost equally ignorant, and reflection teaches us that we know little more of one phenomenon than of the other. We can only say it has been the will of God so to constitute these agents, and that he has shewn us how we may, by labour and application, command them to our uses and benefit. Beyond this we know nothing; and we therefore perceive that these different classes of phenomena alike possess the distinguishing characteristics of a miracle; namely, that they are effects for which we can discern no cause; but there is one understood difference with regard to them, which is the constancy of the one, and the power man has of inducing the other. The sun has risen and set as far back as human tradition carries us; and man, having pretty well found out the necessary conditions, can raise an oak or despatch a telegraphic message as often as he pleases, whereas a miracle is supposed to be an isolated or unfrequent event.

But, in the first place, this difference is more apparent than real; for if the phenomenon possess the main characteristic of a miracle, namely, that

it is an effect without a discernible cause, the re-
petition of the phenomenon does not alter its
character, although, when it is so often repeated as
to become a regularly recurrent phenomenon, we
choose to call it by another name, and pronounce
it a law of nature. Neither does the small part
we have in producing and repeating the second
class of results, in any degree change *their* character. They are still effects for which we can
assign no cause whatever but the will of God, and
are, therefore, as much miracles as if the sun and
the moon suddenly changed places, or we saw
serpents instead of oaks, springing from acorns.

Besides, many phenomena that ultimately become
frequent and common, remain isolated, or unfrequent, till we have so far made ourselves masters
of the secondary causes, and the application of
them, that we can reproduce the phenomena almost
at pleasure ; I say *almost,* for, after all, our incomplete knowledge of the conditions, generally,
introduces an element of uncertainty into the
process ; so that, occasionally, no oak springs where
an acorn has been planted, and our telegraphic

message does not reach its destination, or is imperfectly delivered. God alone is the unerring workman.

It appears, then, that what we call "The laws of Nature," are fundamentally miracles, in which, whoso chooseth to open his eyes, will see the finger of God in operation as much as if the sun had gone "ten degrees backward for a sign," or he had sent down fire from Heaven to consume the earth. And having now, I think, fairly established this position, we will look a little closer at the course nature follows, and endeavour to see how far she is uniform in her results; and at the first glance we perceive that, within certain assigned limits, she allows herself considerable latitude, and that this latitude, in any particular instance, must have appeared to the first observers of it an absolute deviation from her course; and the lower their intellectual standard the more they would feel satisfied that it was so. For example, the first black savage that saw a white man, naturally would conclude him to be an angel, a monster, or the victim of a loathsome disease; and it is highly probable that, if instead of beholding the phenomenon himself, he had only been told of it by one of his comrades, he would have disbelieved the report altogether. We know that a native of the torrid zone could not be brought to believe in the conversion of water into a solid substance, and its reconversion into a fluid, because such a phenomenon was contrary to the laws of nature, as he had learnt them from observation and tradition ; and if he had witnessed this operation performed by a chemist, instead of hearing of it from a traveller, he doubtless would have considered it a miracle or a clever trick. A long catalogue might be made of nature's ordinary phenomena which appeared to the first observers more or less extraordinary, if not a deviation from her laws. But with more extended knowledge we arrive at a larger comprehension of nature, and we can see that she is only uniform within certain limits ; or rather, that it is our ignorance of the conditions which produce these apparent deviations that causes us to think they are such.

The grand operations of nature on which the existence and maintenance of this, our world,

F

depends, God has mercifully kept in his own hands ; and these are so undeviating, that the idea of deviation never enters our minds in connexion with them. In her lesser operations, however, she not only varies with varying conditions, ascertainable or not by us, but she even allows man to interfere, and within certain limitations to alter her course, by the application of new or abnormal conditions ; of which fact the processes of agriculture, horticulture, and the breeding of cattle present the most familiar examples. But these limitations are apparently rigid and impassable. We can convert her bitter and indigestible roots into wholesome and nutritious food, and her acrid fruits into luscious ones ; but we cannot make her acorns produce elms, or her peach trees produce grapes. So we can convert raw-boned, long-horned cattle into short-horned, compact, and fleshy beasts, and we hardly know the limits of her indulgence in these and parallel instances. But we cannot make cows produce sheep, or by any process of feeding procure turkeys from eggs laid by ducks ; and if we were told such a thing had occurred in a remote corner of the world, we should be as incredulous as the black

man or the Siamese Prince ; because, as far as we
are aware, no approach to a similar deviation has
ever been observed.

But what if we were shewn the cow and the
lamb it had produced, or the duck and its offspring the turkey ; and a capable, respectable
person, or several such, who had no interest in deceiving us, asserted that they had actually witnessed the birth of the lamb and the hatching of
the ducks' eggs ; and this even in more than one
instance ?   I think, at first, incredulity would be
pretty general.   It would be said that the thing
was impossible, being contrary to the laws of nature, and that somebody had made these respectable
parties their dupes ; whilst hints would not be
spared in some quarters, that their respectability
even was somewhat questionable.   Physiologists
and scientific persons generally would laugh, allege
the incapacity of untrained eyes and minds for observation, and bestow a liberal allowance of ridi-
cule on the few who had sufficient faith in the
evidence to believe in the prodigy.

But if presently a second instance of the phe-

nomenon was reported to have occurred, and then
a third and a fourth, to the amount of a dozen or
so, apparently, pretty-well-authenticated cases, a
controversy would arise; some continuing reso-
lutely to turn their backs contemptuously on the new
phenomenon, whilst others would set about investigating the evidence or making experiments with
cows, and ducks' eggs. The investigators, except in
a few rare instances of candour, would arrive precisely
at the conclusions they desired; and either find the
evidence good or bad according to their wishes, their
prejudices, their interests, and those of their most
esteemed associates. The hopeful experimentalists
not being able to reproduce the phenomena, would
find themselves the butts of those who were wise
enough to have detected the absurdity at first;
whilst if in a single instance success had been
attained, though it afforded some encouragement
to the believing party, it would be haughtily re-
jected by the other. They, the sceptics, would allege
that the experimentalist had proved himself on
many former occasions a very inaccurate observer,
and that he was extremely credulous, and easily

imposed on.   That it was true the cow had been
shut up in a stable of which he kept the key, and
had been found there by himself in the morning,
with a lamb by her side, and with every appearance
of having brought forth young. But what of that?
It was very easy to procure another key; and there
was no doubt that somebody, for the sake of the
jest, had done so, and, watching the moment of
delivery, had removed the calf and substituted the
lamb; or that the eggs, though hatched in a room
inaccessible to any but himself, had in reality been
changed and coloured.   The believers are silenced,
but not convinced.   No further instance presenting
itself, the controversy dies a natural death, and the
affair is only remembered as a remarkable example
of human credulity, till in the course of time the
world is startled by the announcement that it has been
discovered by an eminent professor that, under certain condititions not yet precisely ascertained, ducks'
eggs may be made to produce chickens!   Whereupon, professors in various parts of the world turn
their attention to the matter; a great deal is written on the subject of poultry, breeding, and feeding;

a learned work is announced from Germany on Incubation ; and a paper is read at the next meeting of the British Association on the anatomical differences between the duck, the turkey, and the hen ; and in process of time it is ascertained that these phenomena had occurred in perfect accordance with an unsuspected law, which, only coming into operation when certain unusual conditions were present, had escaped earlier detection.

Now, whether cows will ever produce lambs, or turkeys be hatched from ducks' eggs, it is impossible for any one now living to say, though certainly the probabilities are greatly against such a result ; but certain it is, that we can only study nature in her own book ; and that when, instead of resorting to that, we resort to our brains to decide whether anything within her domain is, or is not, we are only preparing the canvas for a portrait of ourselves which Titania might have adored, but which the originals have no reason to be proud of.

There is an old adage that has been taken advantage of by those who object to the general diffusion of education, to the effect that a "little learning is a dangerous thing." And this is true, but not in the sense they use it. Education humanises, and a little of it is better than none. But the little learning is dangerous to those who overrate it; and considering how insignificant is the learning of the most learned man that lives; how inevitably ignorant he must be of many things—not only of things unknown to mankind but of things known to other of his fellow-creatures; and how small is the collective wisdom of the world compared to that inscribed in nature's large volume, which God only unfolds to us page by page—it would be wonderful that man should continue so obstinate in his rejection of new truths, did it not evidently enter into God's design to leave him so, for the reasons adduced in the early part of this work. *His* new light is never extinguished however strenuous may be the efforts of its opponents; it is but delayed till time is ripe for its diffusion, and the only sufferers are the wise men—" the disputers of this world," as St. Paul calls them, who persisted in shutting their eyes to it.

It is evident, therefore, that it is by observation

and patient enquiry alone, that we can detect the truth or falsehood of anything asserted to have occurred in nature's domain. Not only so, but it is equally evident that it is only by observation and patient enquiry that we can ascertain the extent of this domain, that is, the extent of her laws. As in the example of the duck's egg, we may reject a thing as contrary to her law which has only occurred under a not before detected law ; and, I think, no one will dispute that there must be thousands of such laws yet to be discovered. Man, in his normal state, is furnished with certain members, and endowed with certain senses and faculties ; but every now and then, we find a human being is sent into the world with a deficiency or superfluity of some of these gifts, we know not why or wherefore. His parents may, or may not be, ordinarily free from disease ; and there may or may not have occurred similar instances in his family ; but in either case, we are not at all nearer an explanation of the phenomenon ; we know nothing whatever about it, and therefore can neither induce or obstruct it. Happily, these distressing cases are not common ; and it may be as well to observe, *en passant*, that they thus eminently fulfil the conditions of a miracle. First, they are rare ; secondly, we do not know at all how such an apparent deviation from nature's laws should arise ; and thirdly, being thus totally ignorant of even the secondary causes, we cannot reproduce or prevent them. There is another peculiarity which we may also note by the way, which is, that as far as we can see, they are not only useless, but worse than useless ; at all events, if the lesson involved in them is a further disclosure of some of nature's deeper secrets—we have not yet learnt it. Nay, we have not even learnt that which lies upon the surface, and which those who run may read, namely, to distrust our own ignorance.

Now man, according to the Scriptures, is a composite being ; and from the same authority we learn that the three constituents of this composite being are, the body, the soul, and the spirit. The investigation of the body lies within the domain of the physiologists who, perceiving mani-

fest advantages to themselves in these researches,
are willing to accept and elaborate every hint that
can throw a light on the subject, so that in this
department we are daily acquiring new and useful
knowledge; but if we enquire what the theologists
have discovered respecting the two constituents
which lie within their domain—the soul and
the spirit—we shall find it to be absolutely nothing. From the Scriptures, however, we may
learn, on the first cursory perusal, that we are
" the Temples of God," that " His Spirit dwells
in us," and that " if any man defile this Temple,
God shall destroy him." These are St. Paul's
words; and he also, in another place, speaks of
the " Spirit which is in a man."

Now, what is the meaning of these words,
" the Temples of God?" words which, like parrots,
we usually repeat after one another without attempting to attach any precise idea to them.
Surely it would be worth while to discover this!
For if God *is* in us, he would probably be not unwilling to help us on many occasions where we
stand grievously in need of assistance; that is, if

we could find him, for it is scarcely to be conceived that he will vouchsafe this assistance while we continue to ignore his proximity.

Suppose any man were told, by what he considered pretty good authority, that he had a friend near at hand who loved him exceedingly, and who was the possessor of enormous wealth and prodigious powers ; I think it is probable that he would spare no pains to ascertain the correctness of the information, in order that he might appeal to this valuable protector whenever his occasions called for aid ; and if he did not do this, I should at once conclude, as I fancy everybody else would, that he placed no faith whatever in the person who had given him the intelligence.

Now, this is precisely our position in regard to the words above quoted, which we read and repeat, and profess to believe. But do we act as if we did ? I think not. There have, indeed, been periods in the world's history when people thought this enquiry not altogether uninteresting. Plato, and the philosophers of his school, and in a later age, what are called " the mystics," were eager to

make discoveries in this direction, and very remarkable are some of their theories and hypotheses. But Plato and his disciples were heathens
and visionaries; and the Mystics were half-mad
enthusiasts, who wandered into all manner of
absurdities while seeking what it was impossible
to find. This, I believe, is the orthodox opinion
of to-day. Plato is read by students, because he
is one of the classics, and his discourse on the soul
is said to be sublime; but I am not aware that it
has induced many researches into the subject of
his essay. Whilst the Mystics, as they are called,
have almost sunk into oblivion, only that the
memory of their teachings and their lives has been
in some degree revived and diffused by a late work
respecting them.

It is true that the disciples of Plato, and the
mystics, who were the disciples of Jesus, did go
astray, and fall into errors and absurdities, as the
disciples of all prophets and teachers of new truths
are ever prone to do: but their object was a grand
one; they were in search of God, and of the
" Light which lighteth every man that cometh into

the world." Whence Plato drew his inspirations
I know not, but can partly guess ; but the Mystics
read the Bible, and sought to find the Spirit in
the letter. However, they became troublesome to
the dominant church, who had occasionally used
them for her purposes, but who, at length, found
it dangerous to countenance their heterodox doctrines. So she denounced them ; and it was time,
when unauthorized teachers pretended to show
man the way to Heaven, and humble apostles of
the new light went about with the Bible in their
hands, and provided only with their scrip and their
staff, aroused mankind to their danger, and preached
salvation without the aid of the church.

Then came Luther, angrily crying, " Will
nothing do for them but Spirit ! Spirit ?" and
who, whilst he diminished the pernicious powers of
the church, and swept away a few of its forms,
swept away the whole of its spirit, leaving the
word " Spiritualist" a term of reproach. And
men, being like sheep, who will follow any leader
bold enough to assume the office, straightway
adopted not only his right but his wrong, and ran

ahead in a new direction.   Whereas nothing
before was too beautiful, too graceful, too rich, too
pompous for the service of God, now nothing was
too ugly, too simple, too plain, too bald, for the
same purpose.   The Almighty, the inventor of
music, the consummate painter, the sculptor who
taught Phidias and Michael Angelo their art, was
supposed to dislike these things ; they were pronounced to be an abomination to him ; and in the
hope of rendering themselves agreeable in the sight
of him who has carpeted his fields with green, and
adorned his garden with many-coloured flowers,
men wore sour faces, cut off the hair he had
himself put upon their heads, and clothed their
bodies in sad-coloured doublets, and slouched hats.
The more ugly and ungraceful anything was, the
better he was conceived to like it ; and the natural
tones of the human voice being considered too
melodious for his ears, they sang to him through
their noses.   All persons who, whether from indifference or a contrary opinion, did not conform
to these practices, were called malignants and
supposed to be doomed to eternal damnation.

Fortunately, time and political changes brought some modification into these views ; if God liked everything that was ugly, man did not ; and when the novelty was worn off, they relapsed into their former customs regarding their persons and other secular arrangements ; whilst, with the exception of some sectarian dissentients, they adopted in their worship a sort of *tertium quid* between the barrenness and baldness of the new era and the pomp and splendour of the old.   Lately there has, indeed, been a limited move in the direction of the former style of ornamentation, and a controversy has arisen that threatens to make considerable havoc in the church.   Men dispute angrily about stoles and candles, and are very hot upon the question of turning their faces to the East or to the West ; volumes are written upon these subjects, and perplexed Bishops and Archbishops are called upon to decide betwixt the disputants.   But there is one most intimately concerned in this matter, whom they never think of consulting, although he must know much better than either party in what manner he likes to be served, or whether one or the other are in the right way to please him; and, according to St. Paul, who, I believe, is held a pretty good authority, he is not very far off, if we only knew how to find him.

But here is a difficulty—a difficulty which has existed in all ages, and in which has originated those fatal mistakes that have caused a large proportion of the misery of mankind since the beginning of the world to this time. All sorts of absurd and mischievous errors, extravagant and pernicious doctrines, ridiculous and even wicked practices, have at different periods prevailed, and have been maintained and enforced with fire and sword, as being in accordance with the will of God. Nay, as having been prescribed by himself to individuals who claimed to hold direct intercourse with him; and who, in many instances, doubtless believed what they asserted, till, at length, from the numerous evils that have been seen to arise from listening to these fallible interpreters, the civilized part of the world have resolved to listen no more; and to go on in the old beaten track, which, though not wholly satisfactory, appears less

dangerous than following possibly deceptive lights
into new ones—and perhaps herein they are wise.
But what must necessarily ensue? Why this, that
since man will not listen to man as the organ of
God's revelations, he is cut off from any sensible
intercourse with God, who remains a name in his
mouth, but has no home in his heart, and retains
little influence over his life—so little, that if man
was "born in sin," as the preachers teach us he
is, this world would be a hell upon earth without
any mitigation.　　But man, though far, indeed,
from being what he ought to be, is still the offspring of God, who, with the patience and loving
kindness of a parent, when one means of instruction fails, has mercifully recourse to another suited to
the age, and the existing stage of human progress.

But it may not inaptly here be asked, Why
should God have thus long withheld information
so needful for us? To this it can only be answered that, judging from what we see, the aggregate of human life is designed, like individual human life, to be progressive ; and that he has his
times and his seasons for everything. That he

G

chooses them wisely, I think, I shall presently be able to shew. With respect to the fallible messengers above alluded to, the answer is, that he reveals himself through human beings who have a certain fitness for the office, but who, being human, are imperfect; and that it is part of our education to weigh and examine the messages they bring by the light of our reason and understandings till we have separated the human error from the divine truth. But instead of doing this, when we accept them at all, we take both together; and the churches, having once adopted the errors, make their stand upon them, and insist that nobody should presume to question their divine origin under pain of damnation. This is, at least, the course we follow with respect to religious revelations; scientific and artistic ones we deal with after a very different fashion.

But human nature is always the same in the main; and the man of to-day is exactly what he was when God is said to have conversed with him on the hill tops; that is, he is liable to error—error wilful, and error accidental; and therefore it is the extreme of folly to accept everything he prescribes without examination, merely because he says God told it him.   And, if we are to yield this implicit belief to one man, why not to another?   What is to be the limit of our abnegation of our own judgment and acceptance of other peoples?   I suppose it would be answered, we are to believe everything included in the Bible, and to give no credence whatever to any man claiming to be a messenger of God, whose words are not there recorded.   But what is our authority for this wholesale rejection?   It cannot be found in the Bible itself; and if it could, what then ?   It might be an interpolation of human error ; and it would be our duty to examine and observe in order to decide whether it were so or not.

But in the midst of all this obscurity and indecision, what is man to do ?   Why, what he has done virtually, though not avowedly—leave God aside, and get on as well as he can without him ; satisfying his conscience by keeping up the simulacrum of external reverence, and instituting certain services to be performed in his honour at appointed periods,

which services, since it happens that the thoughts
and emotions of human beings are very little under
their control, are for the most part coldly and me-
chanically performed, and are more or less weari-
some to those who take part in them. And this
is man's dilemma which he cannot find his way out
of—that he must maintain these hollow institutions
and vapid ceremonies at any price, or the mass of
mankind would not only live wholly without God
in the world, but his very name would scarcely survive in their mouths but as an expletive.

But can these be the services God requires or
desires ? Can they be any expression of the relation in which we stand to him ? I cannot believe
it ; and accordingly many thinking people, viewing
them in the same light, abjure them altogether on
this ground. Now, as I have urged before, if God
has any love or care for his creatures, it is pre-
sumable that when he sees them involved in this
inextricable dilemma, which many perceive, though,
unhappily, still more do not, he will deign to come
to their assistance, and adopt some means of shew-
ing them in what direction they should turn to

find their way out of it. But here, again, is a difficulty ; for man being evidently, within his assigned limits, an independent creature, says—" I will not listen to any more messages from Heaven. They are not to be relied on, and I have no means of testing their authenticity. Moreover, if any man, assuming to be a prophet of God, shall attempt to disturb existing institutions, I shall silence him by putting him into prison, or into a lunatic asylum." And this being indubitably the course we should pursue, if such an event occurred, what remains, but that God should resort to some new method of drawing man's attention to himself?

But how is this to be done, since human speech and pens are no longer accepted organs of the divine messages? And since the world—" the wisdom of the world "—refuses to believe in prodigies or miracles, asserting that the age for these things is past. And this *is* an evident difficulty ; because it has always been observed, and is generally acknowledged, that God works by *means*, and through human or natural agents, and never *immediately* by supernatural fiat. And so strong is man's conviction that it is his will to do so, that he considers it an unquestionable proof of weakness and credulity to believe in any special interference of the Deity, or in the occurrence of any phenomenon out of the domain of nature, or in opposition to her laws, as he has learnt them.

It is quite true, that God might summon the earth to attention by a voice from heaven ; but not to insist on the fact that the earth would be very much terrified, and many of its inhabitants die of the fright, other inconveniences would ensue ; one of which is, that when the generation who witnessed the phenomenon had passed away, the phenomenon would soon cease to be believed in, unless constantly recurring. However, we need not speculate on what would be the consequence of God's doing what we have every reason for believing he never will do. It may be of more use to inquire, what he would be likely to do under present circumstances, and then to cast our eyes around to see if there are any signs of his having commenced this new course of instruction.

Now, it is a remarkable fact that, notwithstand-

ing the determination of the enlightened part of
mankind to withhold their belief from certain kinds
of phenomena, commonly called supernatural, and
which, indeed, cannot be accounted for by any recognized law of nature ; it is, I repeat, a remarkable fact, that in all ages of the world and, as far
as we know, in all nations, there has existed and
still exists an under-current of belief in such phenomena and a persuasion that, in one form or
another, they are of pretty frequent occurrence.
We learn from the Scriptures that, at an early
period of the Jewish history, as well as at the apos-
tolic period, such phenomena were recognized and
that they were rife upon the earth, though doubtless, then, as now, " the wisdom of the world " did
not believe in them.   We find, also, that in what
are called the Heathen nations the same convictions existed, for the same phenomena are recorded in their history, and, indeed, in some
instances, not only the belief in them, but the
practice of invoking them, formed part of the
established religion ; and there were temples, mag-

nificent still in their ruins, which were dedicated expressly to this service.

Other religions of still greater antiquity exhibit traces of a similar faith and practice ; and by some papers lately published in "the Builder," by Mr. Dove, we learn that not only did this belief prevail in the most ancient Eastern nations, but that it is revived amongst that sect of Chinese Religionists now in opposition to the state; the teachings of whose leaders appear to be a sort of Semi-christianity.

More modern examples are not wanting ; not to mention the Rosicrucians and other secret associations for the cultivation of these phenomena, the annals of history show us that they have at divers times appeared spontaneously and in great force, as in the case of the Camisards and Quietists of France, and the witch persecutions of our own country and America. It is to be observed, also, that in both ancient and modern instances, there have always been found a considerable number of persons amongst the enlightened classes who esteemed the evidence adduced for these extraordinary

facts sufficient to warrant belief in them. Insomuch, that it is a matter of wonder in the present
day how so many people of knowledge, sense, and
education, even philosophers and those held to be
amongst the wisest of mankind, could possibly
have given credence to stories so preposterous and
contrary to nature ; and we find this credulity, on
their part, frequently adduced and lamented by
commentators and biographers as examples of
the inherent weakness and fallibility of human
judgment.

But how does it happen that these parties never
suspect their own judgment ? They are human too,
and consequently fallible ; and why are they more
capable of deciding on the existence or non-existence of phenomena, which they have never investigated, or even witnessed, than those persons
who have done both ? I confess I could never
procure any answer to this question except the
following : first, That these things being contrary
to the laws of nature, they cannot happen.   Secondly, that they are of no use ; and it is not to be
supposed that God would break through those

laws and perform a miracle without an object; and, thirdly, That when there *is* any reality in certain abnormal phenomena, they are merely the consequence of disease, and only occur or can be evoked in sickly subjects.

Now, let us examine these three objections, and see what validity we can find in them. To dispose of the first, it is sufficient to answer that man is unacquainted with the laws of nature, and is only beginning to make some progress in acquiring a knowledge of them. Scientific lecturers and essayists are constantly enforcing this fact upon us with a humility which well becomes them, but which would be more to the purpose if it were found present when most needful.

To the second objection, that these phenomena are of no use, and that it is not likely that God would break through the laws of nature without an object, it may be answered that, in the first place, we avowedly know too little of the laws of nature to decide whether the phenomena in question are, or are not, a violation of them, and are therefore, not qualified to predicate anything about their uses, or whether they have any at all. We have not discovered the use of earthquakes, or of tornadoes, or of water-spouts, or of congenital deformity, mental or bodily ; yet, these phenomena doubtless exist and, in the present state of our knowledge, appear not only useless but mischievous.

The third objection, that when there is any reality in certain phenomena they are merely the result of disease, demands a more detailed answer ; although it must be remembered that this objection can only refer to one special class of such phenomena ; I mean such as are purely personal, as clairvoyance, ecstacy, prophetic utterances, or dreams, and so forth.

It is alleged, then, that these phenomena never appear spontaneously, or can be evoked, except in persons more or less diseased, or in weak women and impressionable children ; and as a general fact, I grant at once that this is the one condition that has been yet ascertained. But what of that ? That the secondary cause or disposing condition, is disease, does not alter the fact elicited. Wine

and beer are manufactured through an artificial
process of fermentation, and fermentation is
disease.   It is a step, not only towards death, but
towards corruption ; yet the wine and beer are
facts, nevertheless ; and where natural instead of
artificial fermentation ensues, the product is only
an inferior liquor of the same character.   We
know little about the nature of disease, nor of
the changes that take place in the diseased struc-
tures ; but surely it is not unreasonable to presume
that these changes may, in some degree, alter the
relations between the immaterial and the material ;
and that man, being a composite being, may, in
his totality, be affected more or less by such
changes of structure.   Every change of structure
that ensues from disease must be a step, however
small, towards the death and decomposition of
that structure.   It is true, nature possesses a re-
parative power which art may occasionally slightly
assist ; but if neither nature nor art come to the
aid of the diseased structure, it proceeds, with
more or less celerity, on its way to death and
decomposition ; dragging down with it the whole

edifice.   Whereupon, its inhabitant, the soul, forthwith departs from this falling tenement, and enters
at once, as we are taught, into a new state of
being, and into the possession of new properties
and new endowments, suited to its new circumstances ; that is, it enters into the possession of
those properties and endowments which we believe
to belong to Spirit, and of which we now and
then obtain glimpses from individuals in certain
states of disease, or approach to disorganization.
The glimpses thus afforded us are doubtless very
imperfect, and if looked upon as miracles instead
of natural results, they would, it is granted, appear
absurd and useless.   But the product of the fermentation above alluded to, if incomplete, is of
little value, except, that the observation of it probably first shewed man the way to manufacture
wine and beer ; and is it not possible that the
observation of these despised and ridiculed phenomena might also lead the way to some grand
and useful discovery ?

If so, if such a secret may indeed be evoked
from them—and we do not know that it is not so—

are we in a situation to dispute their existence
without examination, and to condemn them un-
heard, as unworthy of it? Nay more, to brand, as
we do, with the name of impostor or dupe, who-
soever exhibits or professes to have evoked them?

We neither know the boundaries of nature, nor
can fathom the designs of Almighty wisdom. In
God's name, therefore, let us be humble, and study
his works before we pronounce upon them; remembering that, "The base things of the world,
and things that are despised, hath God chosen :
yea, and things which are not, to bring to nought
things that are."

CONCLUSION.

I REMEMBER hearing of a time when sundry persons, denominated lecturers, made a genteel sub-
sistence by driving about the country in gigs, or
one-horse chaises, as I believe they were then
called, and distributing cards announcing that, on
certain terms, they attended schools and private
families, for the purpose of exhibiting the curious
phenomena of a new agent, named Electricity. An
appointment being made, an individual in a black
coat and white choker, duly presented himself,
with a small box under his arm which, being
opened, displayed to wondering eyes a glass cylinder and a few other articles, which he generally
took a long time to arrange, whilst he remarked
that the weather or the atmosphere of the room
was somewhat unfavourable to the success of his
experiments—an intimation judiciously calculated

to abate expectation; adding, however, that he was not without hopes of being able to exhibit something worth the time and attention with which he was honoured.

And this insinuation against the weather or the atmosphere was not without design. It was really a measure of prudence, and prepared his audience to attribute the failures that frequently ensued, to those disturbing causes, and not to the ignorance or imperfect apparatus of the lecturer. He then proceeded to inform them, that an American, called Doctor Franklin, was the discoverer of this new agent, and that he had, by means of a kite, drawn the lightning from the clouds; which fact, of course, filled them with wonder and perplexed their understandings; thus, placing them in a very receptive state of mind, or in other words, exciting their imaginations.

He next announced that, the room being darkened, they would see sparks, and—when everything went well, they did; when there were no sparks, he said there ought to have been, and attributed his failure to the atmosphere or the wea-

ther.   Then followed the grand *coup*—they were
each desired to take hands, and the person at one
extremity of the chain was requested to hold the
wire—a request which some of the party generally
refused to comply with—and, while they stood in
awestruck expectation, the cylinder began to re-
volve.   Suddenly, there was a general scream, and
they all dropped hands ; the lecturer bowed and
smiled with becoming dignity, and the audience
began to laugh and talk over what had happened,
some declaring that they were dreadfully alarmed,
and thought the shock would have knocked them
down, whilst others said that they thought nothing
of it, and scarcely felt any shock at all.

Now, let us imagine a learned professor invited
to this exhibition who, having been in a state of
hybernation for a few years, had not heard of Dr.
Franklin's discovery.   What would he have said ?
Would he have admitted the existence of an unknown, invisible agent, or would he not rather have
attributed the sparks, if he saw any, to some known
chemical action, and pronounced the shock to be
merely the effect of excited imagination, if not the

H

trick of a charlatan ? But suppose the experiments
failed on that occasion, what would he have said
then ? Would he not have attributed the failure
to the effects of his own discriminating eye, which
had disconcerted the performer ? And is it not
possible that this might have actually been the
fact ? The poor lecturer knew very little about
the thing he lived by exhibiting, and his nervous
anxiety to convince the learned professor might
have embarrassed his dexterity, and disturbed the
necessary conditions, by throwing him into a violent state of tremor and perspiration.

Now let us suppose another example. Let us
imagine a native of Otaheite arriving in England
about the same period, with an earnest wish to
know the result of the small pox, which was raging
in his family when he left home, and that the captain of the ship informed him he would procure
the desired information for him in half an hour, if
he would accompany him to a building he saw
yonder. If the Otaheitan were an ignorant savage,
he would never doubt the fact, he would consider
it a branch of " medicine " or conjuring,—in other

words, magic ; because, in his own country, there existed men who pretended to possess certain powers unknown to others ; and, for anything he could tell, the English might be superior adepts in the same arts.

But now let us imagine a " cute " American, instead of a superstitious Otaheitan savage, and that he, on his arrival, never having heard of the marvellous powers of the electric telegraph, was very anxious to learn something of his son, who was settled in Australia, and that the captain of the ship made him a like offer. How he would receive it, I think we can pretty well guess. But, if the captain insisted, and succeeded in procuring the information, would the American believe it, or would he not rather think it a hoax ? But suppose the answer included allusions to circumstances and details unknown to everybody but the father and son, what would be the reflections that would suggest themselves to the " cute " observer ?

In the first place, he would say—" This is impossible, and contrary to the laws of nature, and, therefore, cannot be. It's a lucky guess—a curious coincidence, or, more likely still, they have found out somebody who knows my family; or, I may have dropped something in conversation during the voyage; and they have put this and that together, and so got up the thing for a joke at my expense." And the more intelligent the man was, the greater difficulty there would be in convincing him of their good faith.

But, whenever he did arrive at this conviction, he would arrive at another also, namely, that there must have been an intelligence who answered the inquiry, and who, being acquainted with the circumstances connected with the affair, was qualified to do so, whether it were his son or any one else; and also that there must have been an agent of some sort which conveyed the message across the Atlantic, although he was unable to detect any.

Now, let us apply what I have said to the despised phenomena, called spirit-rapping and table-turning.

Some few years ago, there arrived here an American lady, and we were informed she was a celebrated medium, who had come to England in order to make us acquainted with a new phenomenon which was exciting considerable interest in her own country. She established herself in London, and crowds of people of all characters, and of every shade of opinion and varying degree of intelligence, presented themselves daily in her drawing-room, requesting to know the Christian name of their grandmother, or the precise date at which their great-uncle departed this life. I can take upon me to say, and there is no scarcity of persons able to corroborate the assertion, that, in many instances, they obtained satisfactory answers to these interesting inquiries; but sometimes they got no answers at all, and occasionally they got incorrect ones. Sometimes even no raps were heard, and sometimes there were raps, but no intelligent answers. Naturally, a great controversy arose, those who had been fortunate in their visit were strong on one side, those who had been disappointed were as strong on the other.

Those who had not been at all, reinforced the malcontents, asserting, that Mrs. Hayden was an impostor, and the whole thing a clumsy trick to get money, fit only to impose on the weak and

credulous part of society ; whilst smart young men,
under pretence of a desire to investigate a phenomenon which had engaged the attention of numerous intelligent observers in America, came away
glorious at having outwitted the medium, and disturbed all the conditions under which, it was to be
presumed, such phenomena could be elicited.

Now, it must be admitted that this was not the
sort of investigation most conducive to the attainment of truth ; and although one very qualified
person did condescend to bestow a little attention
to the subject, I take leave to suggest, that it was
rather with the design of dispelling the delusion,
and putting an end to the absurd practice of table-
turning, by the influence of his name, than with
any real desire to ascertain the facts, upon which
he had formed a decided opinion before he commenced the investigation.

Many people, who had suspended their judg-
ments, waiting for further information, considered
this condemnation of the phenomena final, and
enquired no further ; but the convictions of a small
section of observers being undisturbed by this great

authority, they continued to rap and turn tables in
defiance of it ; and have done so with unshaken
faith to the present time.

Now, this being the case, with the additional
circumstances that this section of persevering believers comprises many persons of known and acknowledged intelligence and talent, I hold myself
justified in considering the existence or non-existence
of the phenomena to be still an open question,
hereafter to be decided by fair and conscientious
experiment; and that, in the meanwhile, it is
allowable for any one to offer such suggestions
as may present themselves, as to the possible
character and ultimate design of the phenomena,
supposing them to exist.

With respect to the first question, namely,
the existence of the phenomena, since it must
be a purely scientific problem, I shall only call
attention to the fact, that it is alleged by some
physiologists that the human body appears to
be a sort of Electric Battery, and that if there be
any foundation whatever for this hypothesis, there
will probably be no great difficulty in tracing out

the agency by which concussions may be produced or tables turned.

We may easily conceive such an application might be made of this machine—I refer to the human body—by spiritual power, as to occasion the effects indubitably witnessed; for I am not proposing here to cast any doubt on the fact of tables turning by some unknown agency; of that too many enlightened observers are already fully satisfied. But I only allude to this theory of the physiologists respecting the body, in order to shew that, the secondary cause of tables turning may possibly be the same as that which conveys a message across the Atlantic; and I beg leave to suggest, that the real reason people do not perceive the analogy is, that they are resolved to look upon table-turning as a trick, or an imposture, or a delusion; or, in short, anything but what it is ; namely, a fact unaccountable under the present degree of ignorance as to the possibility of spiritual interference in human affairs.

The reason that man is so unwilling to admit this possibility is, that he mistakes altogether the

nature of spirit and its relation to matter. We
are the offspring of design, and there must be a
designer somewhere no doubt; that there must also be
agents we are entitled to conclude, since we see
that all through nature God works by instruments,
or mediæ ; and that he never, as far as we see,
works by simple volition, or what we call, supernatural fiat.

Now, that tables turn, and something raps, and
draws the strings of the guitar, is certain. I cannot undertake to convince those who are predeter-
mined not to be convinced ; but too many persons
know the fact to make the opinions of those who
do not, of any importance, further than this ; namely,
that they influence the weak and the cowardly, who
have not courage to think for themselves ; and so
strengthen their party by all the ignorance and
cowardice that are ever ready enough to join the
most popular side, that is, the side taken by persons
in authority. Persons in authority, in this case,
being the scientific world, who are not at all disposed to accept phenomena that would overthrow
their theories and declared opinions.

It is true, that Electricity, if admitted as the agent, would fit into these theories well enough ; but what perplexes and irritates them is the *Intelligence* that will by no means be brought to book in the same manner. However, leaving this department of the question aside for the moment, here is a fact, for let them kick as they will, it is one, and they will at last be obliged to admit it, here is a fact utterly rebellious, and therefore wholly inadmissible. What would become of their reputations and associations, if they once admitted the possibility of ignorant men and weak women having succeeded in obtaining results which they, with all their learning, had failed to discover the source of ; and which being no longer able to deny or account for, they must at length confess were produced by a power utterly contemned and ignored by science, namely, *the Spirit*.

I am able to assert, that I have seen tables move without any hand touching them. I have also seen a pair of candles extinguished at the request of the spectators, without being in any way able to conjecture how it was done ; and these things happened in the presence of many intelligent and enlightened enquirers. I have also held a guitar in my hand which was made to produce sounds; chords were struck; and being desired by the invisible Intelligence to sing, I was regularly accompanied through several songs. While I assert these things, I have no expectation of being believed; because if I were, I should be the first person that ever received such a distinction as to be believed when he declared he had seen or heard a fact not recognised by science. Science being an irresponsible power that absolutely rejects all evidence not according with her own views and experience.

I am aware that science is generally right; but she is not infallible. She has made mistakes in her lifetime; and she may rely on it, she never made one more signal, nor more fatal to her pre-eminence, than that she has made in denying, instead of investigating, the phenomena called spiritual manifestations. She knows it too; there are those I could name, who earnestly wish they had not been so hasty in committing themselves; and who see, too late, that there was a great glory to

be won by an early and courageous adoption, when
they had nothing to retract. Now, it is not so
easy ; nevertheless, it must be done, sooner or
later ; and the glory be to him who has the courage
and the honesty first to avow his conversion and
his conviction.

I am far from blaming them for being slow to
adopt so questionable a fact as that of the interference of spirit; spirit being in their vocabulary
and that of many others, both believers and unbe-
lievers, a convertible term for ghost, or, at least, for
the spiritual part, or essential principle, of a deceased
or departed human being. But if they would
condescend to remember, that the essential principle of life, and motion, and of all created things
is spirit ; at least, if they do not hold it to be spirit,
I will thank them to suggest another name for it ;
I say, if they would remember that spirit is the
source of all the vitality, and the cause of all the
existences, and in fact, of all the phenomena, we
are conscious of, perhaps they might not think it
so utterly impossible as they now do, that this ever-
working, all-creating, and all-moving principle,

should choose to offer to man a new exercise and display of its illimitable power ; or that the power which enables us to move our bodies and to lift great weights, by the assistance of our members, might, if it so please, turn tables without our assistance.

Considered in this light, I think it can scarcely be denied that our bodies are merely the vehicles, of a power which, for its own purposes, has chosen to make them so for a certain period ; but that this power could produce every result we see without our aid, if it so pleased.

However this may be, there is indubitably a physical agent, whether that agent be what we are pleased to call electricity, or not. But it is utterly absurd to say, that if it is electricity, there is an end of the enquiry ; as I often do hear people say, who have no more idea of electricity than they have of the joys of Paradise. And if you ask them, " What then is electricity ? How does it produce these effects ?" They refer you to everybody, who, they assure you, knows all about it ! Now, I for one, proclaim that I do not, and I

should be very much obliged to any one who would
tell me all about it. Is it fire? Is it air? Is it
water? Or is it solid matter like the earth? I
declare I do not know, for I never saw it. Will
anybody that has seen it, be kind enough to tell
me? I am quite sure that there must be many
unfortunate persons similarly situated, who would
be equally thankful for the information; and I am
convinced that I have started a question which will
make the fortune of him who can answer it sa-
tisfactorily; only, be it premised, it is a real, solid,
comprehensible explanation I demand; not a tissue
of words which represent nothing but the writer's
or lecturer's own notions, while they leave you entirely ignorant of the main questions, which I
repeat, and maintain, are—What is electricity?
What is galvanism? What is magnetism? What
are imponderables? Where are they, or are they
anywhere? And finally, if they are, what purpose
is there in this constant and persevering conceal-
ment of their whereabouts? I really wish those who
understand such things, and are qualified to instruct us, would answer these questions; because

it occurs to me, that till we have a satisfactory solution of this mystery, we shall never advance far in our knowledge of the use of these agents.

At present, they seem extremely unmanageable and rebellious, and by no means so amenable as they should be to man's authority ; for we are yet uncertain how much they can or will effect at our instigation ; whereas, when acting of their own free will, they seem to be possessed of enormous powers.   For example, we have never yet succeeded in applying electricity to the purpose for which it seems so well adapted ; namely, lighting our cities and houses, and it is not even yet in use as a propeller of ships and locomotives.

Now, I incline to think, that the same power that turns tables could do all this, if properly directed ; but how shall we find out the manner in which this is to be done ? Would it not be possible by studying the phenomena of table-turning to obtain some hints that might be made available ? For example, if tables turn because people unconsciously exert their muscular force, might not the passengers in a railway train be induced to propel the train by the same force, and thus effect a great saving of coals and labour ? The number of passengers that usually travel would afford a muscular power, quite proportioned to the difference between the train and a table.

I merely suggest this, because I am not aware that this unconscious or involuntary muscular force, which, I believe, has been lately discovered, has yet been applied to any useful purpose.

In the mean time, looking upon table-turning as a fact, which it certainly is, I am disposed to think, whether the tables turn by muscular force, or spiritual power, or by any known, though little understood agency—as electricity, for example, that it would be as well to endeavour to ascertain how we can apply the power to other purposes : because, we shall find ere long that, if we do not, somebody else will.   That is, I mean, that if we in England choose to shut our eyes to a patent fact, that only requires to be looked at fairly, to be universally acknowledged, some other nation will get before us.   And as we are the last, generally, to adopt any improvement in science or art, though nobody makes better use of such improvements when once we do move, we had better lose no more time, but begin to study this new force, instead of insulting and reviling the people that exhibit its manifestations.

Men are often persecuted for their religious opinions, or for not having any at all ; but these people are literally persecuted for a natural endowment, be it for good or be it for ill, over which they have no control; and which comes upon them, how or whence, they know not. It is true, they might more or less effectually resist; but are they justified in doing so ? They are wholly ignorant of the source of these extraordinary manifestations, the wise men of the world being entirely at issue on the subject themselves ; some saying they are of heaven, some of hell, and some that they have no existence at all. Now, these people know that they do exist, and until it is decided from what quarter they proceed, I maintain that they are perfectly justified, nay, that it is their bounden duty not to resist a power which may proceed from a holy and heavenly source. At the same time, I

I

do not by any means recommend all the world to fly to table-turning; for I have witnessed too many injurious effects from the practice. Certainly some persons appear to escape any mischievous consequences, while others cannot sit at a circle without unpleasant feelings of one sort or another; and I am acquainted with a lady who cannot even approach a table where people are sitting for manifestations, without experiencing a sensation of numbness and pricking in her arms and hands.

The mediums seem to feel nothing of the kind; and are therefore, I presume, individuals qualified by temperament and constitution to exhibit these phenomena without injury to themselves. I am not aware that any medium has ever suffered from pursuing her calling or vocation, or whatever else it may be denominated.

Before concluding, I must say a few words on another department of this subject, which it is, however, much more difficult to treat, since all must be mere conjecture; and since, moreover, I may expose myself to an accusation of presumption, for venturing to touch upon themes which more properly belong to the theologian. As theologians, however, generally speaking, condemn all enquiry that does not originate with themselves, lest the having recourse to reason, instead of faith, might haply conduct the enquirer to infidelity, I think it is permissible to look into these matters for ourselves, as well as we are able. That any ill consequences can possibly arise from honest and conscientious research after truth, I utterly deny. Certainly we may not find what we seek, but that is no reason we should not make the attempt. If we do not succeed, we are no worse than we were; while, if we do, we shall indubitably be a great deal better—better by all the labour we have expended, and better by the possession of one more of God's truths.

I am of opinion, also, that we may possibly learn, if not what table-turning *is* physically speaking—what it is *not* theologically speaking ; I mean, we may, at least, acquire the certainty that it is not what some people are inclined to think it, namely, an irruption of evil spirits into the bounds of earthly life ; for I hold that such a

I 2

phenomenon as that would be utterly inconsistent with the moral effects hitherto produced. I am myself, indeed, firmly convinced that no such phenomenon is possible under God's government; and I find myself utterly unable to believe that he has so little care of his creatures, as to leave them to contend with such a powerful phalanx of enemies, without other arms than prayer and praise. Because, we see, that prayer and praise are in constant use by the persons most guilty of this practice, and if they are ineffectual preservatives, he has undeniably left us at the mercy of these terrible foes, without any defence whatever. Foes, be it remembered, against whom we have not the ordinary safeguards which our senses furnish—foes invisible and intangible, and whom we must, therefore, necessarily judge by their words. Now, certain it is, that although many of their communications appear to us trivial, they are never immoral or mischievous. On the contrary, it is frequently objected, that it is not likely spirits would come to tell us what we knew before, as that God is good, virtue is commendable, and other platitudes of that description.

However this may be, I think it behoves us to endeavour to ascertain whether the manifestations are produced by spirits, or not; and should it be decided that they are—a fact of which I am free to express my absolute conviction—the next duty imposed on us is, to discover, if we can, the object and purpose of so remarkable a visitation, occurring at a period in which the belief of spiritual intervention in earthly affairs is wholly scouted.

Let us now suppose, that the governor of this universe, whom we call God, found that man was going far astray, and that owing to the degree of enlightenment and civilization he had attained, he had ceased altogether to believe in what we denominate the supernatural. That in consequence, also, of various circumstances, such as those I have alluded to in my first chapter, he had, on mature deliberation, resolved to credit nothing that appeared contrary to what he conceived to be the ordinary laws of nature; and that being too ignorant and conceited to be aware how little he knew of these laws, he was quite satisfied to believe that every apparently supernatural phenonenon, was an impossibility and an absurdity, fit only to delude the weak and superstitious. Suppose then, man was so rash as to say, " God never interferes with us ; he has placed us here to get on as we can, but as for helping or directing us out of our difficulties, it is the last thing he would think of. We indeed, are told, and some of us believe, that at one period, things were different ; but if ever this was the case, the idea of such interference in modern times is scouted even by theologians ; while we have abundant proof that everybody who conceives himself inspired, is only a madman or a rogue, and that his proper place is the lunatic asylum or the jail."

Now, man having arrived at this conclusion— for my picture is drawn from the life—what is it to be supposed that God would do, if he wished to make some communications to man that deeply concerned his temporal and eternal welfare ? Is it not allowable to think, that he would draw his attention, first, by phenomena, apparently unprecedented, which, being contrary to the recognized laws of nature would appear to some supernatural,

and to others impossible? Thus, all would be
awakened, more or less; for the scoffers must end
by being convinced, if it be his will that they
should be so.

If this is not an utterly absurd hypothesis, let
us admit it for a little; and proceed to consider
what might result from such a course on the part
of the power that rules our destinies.

In the first place, we must suppose, that by
this unusual effort to command our attention, we
are on the eve of some tremendous revolutions for
good or for ill; and that if we do not choose to
give ear, we may either suffer a great evil or
escape a great good. Now, which it is, no man
can say; but if I may be permitted a rash conjecture, I am inclined to think it is the latter. As
I before remarked, we have attained a degree of
civilization unknown, as we believe, at any earlier
period of the world's history. A corresponding
progress has been made in the arts and sciences,
although with respect to some departments of the
latter, it is true, we are rather retrograde than ad-
vancing. However, in the main, we are advanced,

and we believe also, that there are other symptoms of progress and perfecting that are still more important. Wars, if not less bloody, are less savage. Men—few men at least, take the life of a fallen foe ; and those who do so, are considered out of the pale of civilization.

There is another thing not less remarkable, which is, the general desire for more equality in the distribution of those advantages which are derivable from education. I do not mean merely education itself, but I allude to those advantages which do not trench on the rights and privileges of the upper classes—the rich and well-born, for I am far from believing that any real advance is made, or likely to be made, towards that equality which forms the ideal of too many well-intentioned and enthusiastic individuals ; who do not consider that God himself has clearly ordained inequality, since the endowments of nature are so infinitely various in kind and degree ; for unless these endowments were alike and equal, all equality of fortune and condition must be utterly impossible and unattainable, even in the most moderate form.

We should consider that God, who has made us
what we are, is the best judge of his own purposes ;
and we should consider also, that if he has not
made us equal here, there may be an adjustment
hereafter ; and that to fight and squabble for
equality, is a clear contravention of his evident
designs.

But if in certain relations we must remain un-
equal, and if in the endowments of nature he
reveals his intention that we should be so, there is
no reason why the poor, the weak, the sick, or the
lunatic, should have their misfortunes aggravated
by the neglect or haughty indifference of the more
fortunate members of society ; and I think the
solicitude displayed on this subject by many persons
in high places, is the best possible sign of the
times ; and it is the one on which I found a rational hope, that the period is arrived when we
shall receive farther aid from God himself.   And
this hope has emboldened me to write this little
book, by which I may possibly succeed in drawing
attention to phenomena much more extraordinary and significant than those can conceive

who have refused to examine them. It is vain to insist on what so many know, what so many have felt, what so many have seen ; but this I will say, that those who refuse to witness these manifestations—if even as a matter of curiosity—lose, I think, a considerable gratification. No doubt, there is often disappointment or imperfect, and, to strangers therefore, suspicious circumstances, attending these displays ; but frequently, very extraordinary things occur ; and I cannot imagine any reasonable creature seeing what takes place on such occasions, without desiring to ascertain, at least, the mode of the deception, if he think it is one.

So much for the manifestations and the possible agent which effects them ; now I must beg leave to say a few words on the subject of the intelligence that directs the needle or the hand of the telegraph, indicating the letters necessary to form a word or a name.

I have observed that we are spirits, ourselves, encased or incarnated in fleshly bodies, for a special purpose no doubt. What that purpose is, it is not, at present, my intention to enquire; but so it is; and if we are spirits, we must be suffering some degradation, because our intelligence, which is limited by the periphery of these bodies, is far short of what spirit unincarnated must enjoy.

Now, I conceive that this limitation is the source and origin of all evil—that is, of all the evil by which we suffer. No doubt, there may be other ill influences; but it is not necessary to seek them, for in this limitation we find an absolute and entire explanation of every ill that flesh is heir to; since, did we know all things, we might undoubtedly enjoy that perfect happiness which we are told is to be the portion of the just hereafter. It is because our knowledge is so limited, that we err in every department and relation of life; and I am so satisfied that this is the origin of all our misfortunes and sins, that I shall not pause to dilate further on this branch of my subject, but proceed to enquire how we may escape the consequences of this limitation.

We know, or at least believe, as I have observed above, that spirit unincarnated and free, must

possess faculties and privileges far beyond those we
enjoy ; and we, moreover, learn by several incidents
related in the Scriptures, that God employs the
spirits of the just in assisting and protecting
human beings.   There are many people, doubtless,
who think this a fable ; but, at all events, let us
admit it as a fact, for the sake of argument.   Well,
if this be so, there is no doubt that, practically,
the belief in the possibility of this valuable assistance is lost ; and the assistance itself, if offered,
would be rendered utterly nugatory, because man
has become so convinced of the non-intervention
of spiritual with earthly life, that he rejects as folly
and absurdity every approach to a belief in such
intervention ; and brands with the name of superstition, every practice that countenances such a
faith.

Let us now see first, how far this wholesale rejection is warranted ; and secondly, whether the
experience of mankind in general, would not lead
us to a directly opposite conclusion.

I presume there are very few people in the
world who have not, at some period or other, found

themselves almost miraculously preserved from a threatening danger; their preservation from which seemed to be owing to some sudden and wholly unpremeditated act or movement on their own part. I can positively say, that three such instances live in my memory, in each of which I was, in this manner, incomprehensibly saved from death. Every one of these instances occurred long before the Spirit manifestations had been heard of; and even before I had been led to turn my attention to the existence and possible proximity of the spiritual world. I was, if not as unbelieving, at least, as indifferent as anybody, to ghost-stories; and what interest I felt in them was, I must confess, entirely due to a natural love of the marvellous—that unfortunate faculty which wisdom designates as the root of so much folly. I was, moreover, an utter disbeliever in what is called " special providences ;" because, I urged, if providence interferes to save one person in a sinking ship, why did he not save all the rest ? In short, I was a disciple of that excellent and wise man, George Combe ; who saw 'farther into truth, I believe, than most men that have lived upon this earth, and did more for mankind, in teaching them to obey the natural laws, than all the preachings and sermons that have been delivered since Adam first led us astray, by listening to the fascinations of a beautiful woman, who wished him to eat of the tree of knowledge, and so suddenly and un-fairly obtain that which he had not laboured for. The story of Eve and the apple, which is most absurdly admitted into the sacred writings, being accepted as a circumstantial account of what is called the " Fall of Man," appears to me not only foolish, but blasphemous ; for there can be nothing culpable in desiring knowledge, and though we are told, God had forbidden them to eat of that tree, they must necessarily have been too ignorant of right and wrong to be sensible of the amount of their fault. Two people, born and living alone in a garden, with all their wants supplied, could have no notion that to eat an apple was a sinful act, because, they probably ate apples every day ; and one apple being very like another, it was natural they should imagine the only difference between this

and the rest was, that it was pleasanter food.   In
short, they were exactly in the position of children,
forbidden to pluck the fruit of a particular tree ; like
children, they disobeyed ; not because they desired
knowledge, for they could have no idea what knowledge was, but because the fruit being forbidden, it
naturally awakened their attention and cupidity.

Now the belief that mankind have ever since
been suffering untold evils in consequence of this
peccadillo of Eve's, is too childish for any rational
creature to entertain ; but in this allegory, I think
I see a meaning lurking under the disguise of a
fable, that may really concern us ; for there is no
doubt, that the allegory is very ancient, and be-
longs to the earliest periods of man's inhabiting
the earth.

Suppose we consider Eve as the type of an unholy desire for things unattainable in this life ;
suppose again, we take Adam as the type of honest
and persevering industry, that is content to work
for what he wishes to enjoy.   Now Eve invites
him, by an act of disobedience, to possess himself,
per saltum, of that which he is endeavouring

patiently to acquire by the sweat of his brow, and the labour of his hands, or brain, as it may be. Had Adam refused, I opine he would have acted wisely; because all experience shews us, that sudden gains are not the most beneficial to man. Premature children, prodigious geniuses, too rapid accessions to wealth or power, are all apt to turn to bitterness.   I do not say there are no exceptions, but this is undeniably the rule.

But, to return from this digression, let us ima-gine, that at some very early period of the world's history, men thought differently with regard to the possibility of spiritual communion, that is, that they believed it not only possible, but that they looked upon it as amongst the ordinary phenomena of human life ; and, moreover, that they were aware of their being placed under the protection of some intermediate beings, whose office it was to instruct them in the ways of this earthly life, of which they had had experience themselves ; and with the dangers and difficulties of which they were therefore fully acquainted.   Imagine, again, that these spirits, retaining some tincture of earthly yearnings, had allowed themselves to be seduced by man into a premature revelation of things which it was not intended by providence he should know till he had fulfilled his appointed task, and thereby qualified himself for the possession of such high knowledge—knowledge which, very probably, would unfit him for his progress through this pilgrimage, which is doubtless designed to induct him into a higher and more exalted state of being.

Now, if for the sake of argument, we admit this hypothesis, we see at once, that the natural consequence of such disobedience must be, that the privilege of spiritual communication would be forfeited, or at least, only permitted in such rare instances as those in which the character and conduct of a human being might exempt him from sharing the penalty. Moreover, that these exceptions, being so *very* exceptional, must be purchased by a life of much suffering, perhaps, even supererogatory suffering—which supposition may possibly offer the true explanation of an idea which has prevailed in all the most ancient religions of the East ; and which still survives more or less, in every religion,

K

namely, that voluntary and self-inflicted pain, or
abstinence, were meritorious and pleasing to divine
providence. Herein, also, we might find the true
interpretation of "the sins of the fathers being
visited on the children;" for, doubtless, ages must
elapse ere the memory of these unholy commun-
ings and the desire for them would be lost and
extinguished; and thus we see, that the sufferings
of mankind may have actually been the natural
consequence of the sins of their forefathers; and
that the story of Adam and Eve, though not a
literally, may be an allegorically, correct account of
how man fell from the privileges of his birthright.
The stringent laws against magic and witchcraft,
which formed part of all ancient codes, may be
similarly accounted for; as also the universal persuasion that a dealing with spirits was both un-
lucky and unholy.

Now, I believe, though it may seem presumptuous to say so, that this is the real meaning of
what we call the Fall of man; and that the period
having arrived, when not only the memory but the
desire for Spiritual communication is wholly extin-

guished, we may look for a gradual restoration or reinstatement; and that this is moreover, the true meaning of what is called the Millenium, or the reign of peace and good-will upon earth.

Should this be the case, I need not suggest to the intelligent reader, all that therein must be included. He will see it at one glance.   And he will see, also, how needful the assistance of our spiritual friends has become, at a period when life has grown into a struggle and a contention for material existence that threatens to disorganize society, and render all the restraints of morality and religion utterly nugatory, perhaps even incompatible with worldly prosperity.   And yet this is a condition that man will always aim at; and, no doubt, was intended to aim at; since, without such an incentive, it would not have been possible, constituted as he is, to induce him to labour, and thus promote the well-being of others, as well as his own.

We see, also, that idleness *is* a sin; and that work, of some sort, is man's duty as well as his interest.   By work alone, can he procure that kind of prosperity that is truly conducive to happiness;

and we see constantly, that those who are born to live without labour, either make some for themselves, or seek in violent exercise and active sports a substitute for it—a poor substitute, it is true; but still, better than none—where the sport is innocent—which unhappily it often is not; for man, heedless of any sufferings but his own, is utterly insensible to those of, what he is pleased to denominate, " the lower animals."

Perhaps, if we knew all, we should not be so heedless of these suffering creatures, who are certainly endowed with faculties, of some sort, that we are unable to comprehend, and which we call by the name of instinct; pronouncing it much inferior to reason. Now, I should like to know, who could construct a honeycomb out of the pollen of the flowers, or build a bird's-nest without hands? Reason is a very valuable endowment certainly; but till it can teach us the way to truth, it is quite evident that, either we do not know how to use it, or that it is not so supreme a gift as the despised gift of instinct.

The discovery of Truth is evidently as much

our appointed task, as the construction of a honeycomb is the appointed task of the bee. He performs
his with unerring sagacity, and has done so as far
back as tradition carries us; whilst we are yet
floundering in mire and filth, because we are too
cowardly to begin ours, or even to look it straight
in the face.

It is not my province to point out all the absurdities, and contemptible temporisings and evasions,
into which this odious pusillanimity leads us ; but
this I will say, that never since the world began,
were these vile compromises with truth more rife,
or more pernicious, or more inexcusable, than they
are at present. We have multitudes of books, and
multitudes of writers, and, I may add, abundance
of talent; but how few dare brave the sneers of
the world and the persecutions of the Religious
part of it, by speaking out what they think and
believe to be the case—namely, that we are living
in a lie ; and that the Bible, though full of most
valuable teachings, is not the absolute and indis-
putable word of God ! How few will venture to
draw man's attention to the fact, that though we

believe in the main history and instruction, we are obliged to make a compromise with truth; and for the sake of what we do believe and see the use of, to continue insisting on people's accepting what is evidently, either irrelevant or interpolated matter, the offspring of human error, ignorance, and superstition.

I am well aware, that I shall raise an outcry by this assertion; but I think, when the outcry is over, and people begin to reflect, they will find that I have not advanced anything more than they have frequently admitted to themselves, and to those with whom they could confidentially converse on such a subject. Now I beg leave to ask, why any-body should withhold what he or she not only believes to be true, but what is generally acknow-to be so? Only not in public, because in public would be found many persons who desired to leave these errors untouched, since they apprehend, that if any part of the sacred volume were pronounced not infallible, the whole would lose its authority; and so man be left without any Spiritual guide whatever.

I confess I have no such apprehension. On the contrary, I believe that the Bible contains hints of such value, and of such vital importance to man's welfare and happiness, that nothing can ever destroy its influence ; and so far am I from apprehending such a calamity, that I believe the book would be much more widely esteemed and respected, and much more extensively studied, if we cleansed it of its errors ; because these errors being such as impair the solemnity and deduct from the Spiritual character of the volume, they repel many who would otherwise be attracted by its beauty and the instruction it affords.

But I am exceeding the limits of my task, and I must draw this little book to a close; but before I say farewell to my readers, I will venture to ask one question, answer it who can.

This question I have repeatedly asked myself and others ; but I confess, though amongst these have been some of the first men of the present age, I never yet obtained a satisfactory answer, or, at least, any answer that told me more than I knew before. My question is this : Why do the planets always maintain the same invariable course, and never by any accident forget the road they are to take ? We are not disposed to fancy these globes possessed of intelligence; and moreover, some of them we believe to be inhabited, like our earth, and therefore, we presume, are similarly constituted bodies. Insomuch, that we may venture to predicate that it is not their own volition or consciousness that guides them through their heavenly journey.

Now, we must consider, that tables turning, and rapping, may appear very insignificant operations, but that the purpose of these insignificant operations may be a very important one, namely, no less than convincing mankind that the fact of Spiritual interference in human affairs is both possible and true. We are at present wholly ignorant how this operation, is performed though several ingenious theories have been started on the subject; as that the Mediums crack their toes or their knee joints; and I believe one enquiring person has actually detected a lady in cracking her hip joint. However this may be, there is no necessity in the

world for having recourse to such an expedient to
produce raps, or that we should seek in involuntary
muscular pressure an explanation of table turning;
for we have only to recall the circumstance that
the Earth and the planets turn by what is called
gravitation, to be satisfied that the tables may turn
by the same force, and that the power which has
generated this force and keeps it in constant operation, may choose to apply it to lesser manifestations.

Sir Isaac Newton founded his grand and com-
prehensive theory on a very trivial incident; but
he discerned at once that from the lesser he might
ascend to the greater; now, let our philosophers
consider whether he would not have been disposed
to descend again from the greater to the lesser, had
he been alive now and heard that tables were
competently asserted to move without any visible
cause ?

I, for my part, think that he would; and I
think, moreover, that when he had ascertained the
fact that they did so move, mankind would have
endeavoured to discover how this force might be

applied to some useful purpose. He is gone hence ;
but if the departed do overlook our doings here, I
really think he must be amazed at our obtuseness
and incapacity for observation—a faculty, by the
way, which our scientific men appropriate wholly
to themselves. On this occasion, however, they
have certainly yielded their pre-eminence to the
" weak and foolish," as St. Paul calls us ; for it is
women and unscientific persons that have hitherto
carried out these experiments, and satisfied themselves of their soundness.

Now, I am well aware that mistakes are often
made, and that people find what is called mare's
nests ; that is, they find something they do not
understand, and forthwith adopt conclusions which
are overthrown by further investigation. But this
folly or weakness is by no means peculiar to women
or unscientific people; on the contrary, it seems
to me that it is extremely rife amongst the learned
themselves. For example, we have been told all
manner of extraordinary things about electricity—
first, that it was a fluid, then that it was an im-

ponderable, and now that it is neither one nor the other, but only a force.

What the word "force," so employed, may mean, I really have no idea; but perhaps some learned professor will tell me.   Is it a thing to be seen, felt, or understood, as the grammar has it ? If not, how did they become aware of its existence ? I suppose they will answer, "We became aware of its existence by the effects we observed it to pro- duce."   But suppose I choose to dispute the ex- istence of these effects—What then ?

Why, they will very naturally say that I am an ignorant, conceited idiot! And so I should be ; for, although I have never witnessed the operations of this agent, otherwise than as exhibited in lecture rooms by somewhat incompetent performers, I have no doubt that the accounts I hear from so many people who can have no possible interest in deceiving me, are substantially correct.   But if I believe what the scientific world asserts in regard to this invisible agent, why will not the scientific world believe what I assert in regard to table- turning ?   "Because," say they, "you are not a

competent observer. You believe your eyes and
ears, and are not aware that they are utterly fallacious guides to truth."

Am I then to conclude that science has some
special faculty for the discernment of truth, which
we less fortunate members of society are destitute
of ? Or, must I not conclude that this faculty is
merely the result of senses trained to observation
and analysis; and that, consequently, I, or any
other moderately endowed individual, might acquire
by practice and industry, the same degree of dis-
crimination ? If so, why do they reject the evidence
of numerous intelligent persons who, for aught
they know, may be quite as well qualified as themselves for detecting imposition, and pronouncing on
the genuineness of the spiritual manifestations ?

I answer, because they are resolved not to believe in the operations of spirit, and because they
are utterly without any instinctive feeling of their
own spiritual origin; in short, because, though
not avowedly, they are practically, materialists. I
do not by any means use this as a term of reproach.
Far be it from me to reproach any man, or set of

men, for holding opinions which have been honestly formed ; but I do say, that, having arrived at
the conclusion that all is matter and organization,
and what they call the laws of nature, if they persist in shutting their eyes and ears to everything
that may open out to them higher views, they incur
a fearful amount of responsibility ; since it is not
only their own understandings they stultify and
pervert, but those, as I have said before, of all
the weak and cowardly people who listen to their
voices with childish deference, and even refuse to
believe their own senses in obedience to their com-
mands.

Once more I assert, that whether these manifestations be from heaven or hell, or whether they
exist at all or not, is a question that we have every
right to ask of those who, having qualified themselves for investigation, are bound to answer. If
the weak and foolish part of the world are wrong,
let them be set right on some better grounds than
bare denial ; if it should so happen that they are
right, why then let us all thank God that he has
bethought himself of our great need, and has

condescended to send us aid before conceit and ignorance have drawn down upon us a new and more fearful curse than the last—namely, an utter loss of his favour and countenance.

We are told that there is a sin unpardonable by God himself—the sin against the Holy Ghost, which must mean the sin that destroys and abrogates all connection with the Spirit of God. Now, I believe that this sin is virtually if not actually, committed by many, unconsciously; and therefore, we must hope that it will not be accounted to them. What is the meaning of a man's saving his soul alive? Is it not preserving it from being cut off from that divine fountain of grace that constantly flows into those who are willing to receive it?

I believe this is the real meaning of words which are often heard in our churches, but which I never happened to hear explained. When theologians can offer any better interpretation of them, I shall be happy to accept it; but in the meantime, let them bethink themselves that, if it should be as I believe, namely, that God is offering us an open door to the recovery of our birthright, what weight of responsibility must be theirs, who not only refuse to enter themselves, but forbid the souls committed to their charge to do so likewise?

THE END.

BILLING, PRINTER AND STEREOTYPER, GUILDFORD, SURREY.

For EU product safety concerns, contact us at Calle de José Abascal, 56–1°,
28003 Madrid, Spain or eugpsr@cambridge.org.

www.ingramcontent.com/pod-product-compliance
Ingram Content Group UK Ltd.
Pitfield, Milton Keynes, MK11 3LW, UK
UKHW012339130625
459647UK00009B/401